THE MORAL DIMENSIONS OF INTERNATIONAL CONDUCT

The Jesuit Community Lectures: 1982

THE MORAL DIMENSIONS OF INTERNATIONAL CONDUCT
The Jesuit Community Lectures: 1982

Edited by James A. Devereux, S.J.

 GEORGETOWN UNIVERSITY PRESS
Washington, D.C.

ISBN: 0-87840-406-6

Library of Congress Cataloging in Publication Data:
  Main entry under title:
  The Moral Dimensions of International Conduct
  Contents: The conduct of affairs between the Western democracies and the
Soviet Union / Shirley Williams — The relationship between rich nations
and poor / Denis Goulet — Human rights and the moral dimensions of interna-
tional conduct / José Zalaquett — [etc.]
    1. International relations—Moral and ethical aspects—Addresses, essays,
lectures. I. Devereux, James A.
JX1255.J47   1983   172'.4   83-11660
ISBN 0-87840-406-6

CONTENTS

Introduction   1

SHIRLEY WILLIAMS

The Conduct of Affairs between the Western
Democracies and the Soviet Union

Five Questions   7
Two Views of the Soviet Union   7
An Ideal that Failed   9
The USSR and the Third World   12
Challenge to the West   13
Beyond Nationalism   16

DENIS GOULET

The Relationship between Rich Nations and Poor

Means and Ends in Development   27
Bankruptcy of Development Paradigms   30
A Crisis of Imagination   39
Domestic Roadblocks to Development   44

JOSÉ ZALAQUETT

Human Rights and the Moral Dimensions of
International Conduct

Values and Interests   63
The Evolution of Human Rights   64
Toward Universal Norms for Human Rights   68
Whose Responsibility Are Human Rights?   74

J. BRYAN HEHIR

The Use of Force and the International System Today

Force, Morality and Nuclear Weapons   85
The Real World: Bipolar or Interdependent?   85
Catholic Teaching on the Use of Force   89
The Church in the Nuclear Age   93
The American Church and the Nuclear State   97
The Purpose of the Pastoral Letter   101

*This publication has been made possible
by the Georgetown Leadership Seminar
and the Jesuit Community of
Georgetown University*

INTRODUCTION

Over the entrance to the hall at Georgetown University where these lectures were delivered is this inscription from Teilhard de Chardin: "The age of nations is past. It remains for us, if we do not wish to perish, to set aside the ancient prejudices and build the earth."

The sentiment is striking but, for some at least, not altogether satisfying. Most of us are attracted to the ideal of human solidarity that these words imply. Many of us believe that our race is a single family, and that all of us who inhabit this planet are brothers and sisters under God. We are ready to deplore on moral grounds the excesses of nationalism. None of us is in favor of the arms race. We are appalled by an international economic system that leaves millions of children half fed or not fed at all. We condemn nations that make the abuse of the human person an everyday instrument of government.

But how can Teilhard's call to set aside the prejudices of nationalism and build a new earth be answered in realistic practice? Is it even safe to do so? How can we enter into fraternal partnership with nations whose own practice is to enslave rather than to build humanity? Is it possible to set aside the ancient prejudices? Are they not the givens of international politics—the assumptions on which realistic strategies of conduct must be based? Certainly, for Machiavelli and his latter-day followers the acts and policies of sovereign states are governed by no higher law than that of self-interest. Yet for all its claim to realism, many today find this view unacceptable in principle and ruinous in its consequences for humanity. They look for a better answer.

Such a search ought to take place at Georgetown, first because it is a university long engaged in the study of international relations, and second because it is a Catholic university called to reflect upon the human condition in the light of Christian wisdom. In order to promote this search, the Jesuit Community at Georgetown invited four distinguished people to lecture on specific aspects of international conduct and its moral dimensions. Besides a Roman Catholic background, each lecturer brought a special perspective to the task. Shirley Williams is a Member of Parliament in Great Britain and a founder of the Social Democratic Party. Her reflections on the conduct of affairs between the West and the Soviet Union reveal the practicing politician whose assumptions are rooted in Christianity. Professor Denis Goulet, who holds the O'Neill Chair of Education for Justice at Notre Dame University, is a leading specialist in development economics. He examines the dilemmas of the poverty and wealth of nations, and cautions against solutions that introduce new problems for developing peoples. José Zalaquett brings to his topic, "Human Rights and the Moral Dimensions of International Conduct," a unique experience. He is an exile from political oppression and a former chairman of the executive committee of Amnesty International, a group that has enjoyed remarkable success in the defense of fundamental human rights. J. Bryan Hehir's lecture on the use of force between nations reflects his experience as an architect of the United States Catholic Bishops' recent pastoral letter on the morality of nuclear warfare.

Our purpose, then, and our hope in presenting these lectures is to focus attention on the moral dimensions of international conduct. A word about their occasion. In the fall of 1982 Georgetown University dedicated a splendid new building to house those of its programs that cut across cultural and national boundaries. The building was named after the University's forty-third president, Edward B. Bunn, S.J., a priest of broad vision and deep Christian love. It was to celebrate that event that the Jesuit Community at Georgetown sponsored these lectures. The community now dedicates this volume that gathers them together to the happy memory of Father Bunn.

JAMES A. DEVEREUX, S.J.

SHIRLEY WILLIAMS

The Conduct of Affairs between the Western Democracies and the Soviet Union

Shirley Williams is an author and a founding member of the Social Democratic Party. At the time this lecture was given (October 5, 1982), she was a Member of Parliament for Crosby.

FIVE QUESTIONS

Let me begin on this very important subject, which I'm conscious of being unable to contribute as much to as I would wish, by asking five questions. The first of those questions is, What is the nature of the Soviet Union? Is she fundamentally an aggressive country or fundamentally a defensive country? The second question is, What challenge does her political and economic system pose to our democracies? And I don't mean that just in terms of military challenge; I also mean it in terms of a political and even a spiritual challenge in the deepest sense of that word. What challenge does it pose to the countries of the Third World? What is the best approach to adopt? And here, I think it would be worth distinguishing between the very different approaches of different Western allies. Finally, what steps can be taken to improve our relationships without damaging our interests? That last question will take me into the much wider areas to which Father Devereux referred in quoting the remarks of Teilhard de Chardin, namely the question of what sort of world structure we can create in what is a profoundly divided world.

The last of those questions, what steps can we take to improve our relationships with the Soviet Union without damaging our interests, is when I think about it, a very European question, because it begs the goal of whether or not we think it is right or wish to improve our relations. It could be argued that we do not want good relations, that the ideological chasm is so deep that it would be better to remain on either side and not try to reach across it. You will therefore appreciate that I am already to some extent reflecting what is a more general Western European view in assuming that we do want as good relations as we can get, even with this regime, many of whose actions merit our disapproval.

TWO VIEWS OF THE SOVIET UNION

At the present time, then, let me begin with the question, What is the nature of the Soviet Union? At the present time there is less dialogue between the United States and the Soviet Union, in particular, than there has been at almost any time since the end of the Second World War. It is true that arms negotiations, or rather, arms control negotiations have recently resumed: the INF talks in Geneva, the START talks and so forth. Nevertheless, the degree of intellectual and civil interchange between the United States and the Soviet Union is probably at its lowest ebb in a very long time. That flows in part, I think, from a viewpoint and a set of conclusions held by the present

American administration. But it can also be traced to the much more forward position taken by the Carter administration which believed that there was a rather specific moral platform that needed to be adopted vis-à-vis the Soviet Union, and I refer specifically to the moral platform of human rights. The Carter administration unquestionably put the Soviet Union in an embarrassing position because it insisted upon pursuing the question of human rights, because it treated the Helsinki Agreements very seriously, because it raised difficult questions which many politicians in world affairs do not like to hear asked insistently. In doing so, of course, it got itself, as any Western democracy will do, into considerable problems on the question of double standards. How far do we ourselves apply principles of human rights to those countries considered our allies, I mean our own dictatorships and our own friends who embrace racist and, in other human rights terms, unacceptable attitudes?

It is quite clear that in many ways the Soviet Union is more comfortable with an approach that is based upon *realpolitik*, like the one the Nixon administration, and its distinguished Secretary of State, Henry Kissinger, adopted in their attitude toward relations between the great powers, an attitude that most things were negotiable, that those negotiations depended upon a hard assumption about the separate national interests of the individual countries and of the alliances, and that it was inappropriate and indeed in many ways unhelpful to get involved in ideological and moral questions. It is perfectly true that the United States, more than, I think, any other significant world power, with the possible exception of India, has moved rather uneasily between believing that foreign policy should be infused with a sense of morality and believing that foreign policy is a matter essentially to do with the realities of interchange and communication between nations. Indeed, one could say of the United States that it moves from trumpet to lyre and doesn't always make it easy for the rest of the world to know where it is. That isn't a criticism; in many ways I believe it is admirable that the United States believes there ought to be a moral dimension in foreign policy. I think the problem for many of us is that sometimes that moral dimension is interpreted in very simple ways, in black and white terms, and is very often seen from the point of view of those who don't perhaps always fully appreciate the extent to which history and geography have determined the point of view of other countries.

Let me now apply these ideas to the Soviet Union. In doing so, I am rather posing questions than suggesting that there are any simple answers, since that is the purpose of these lectures as I understand them. One view of the Soviets, and it is one, I think, held more in the

United States than in Western Europe (though my own Prime Minister would certainly have a good deal of sympathy with it), is that the Soviet Union is an ideological and strategic enemy; that she is an aggressive country, determined to export the Communist Revolution wherever she conveniently can; that she would wish to destroy everything for which our own democracy stands, be that British belief or family values, or the acceptance of Christian and Jewish civilization, or the concept of such things as human rights to which I've referred. In short, and to put it in its most extreme form, this viewpoint sees the Soviet Union as a kind of anti-Christ.

I think the alternative view, the softer view, is one that is much more colored by history. It is the view that you will find more frequently held in Bonn or Paris or on the part of opposition groups in London; and it holds that, increasingly, the Communist Revolution is becoming absorbed in the eternal geographical objectives and aims of the Russian state. For, in many ways, as one looks at the history of Russia, and I use the word Russia advisedly, one sees a similar pattern, a pattern of a neurotically defensive country that is constantly looking around its borders to assure that its neighbors are friendly, that is profoundly concerned, in particular, about its border with China, that is only too happy to take an advantage but will step back when the risks become great, that is extremely suspicious and fearful of Germany because of the colossal price its population paid in the Second World War. It is a country that probably has a genuine fear and hatred of war, not because it is uniquely a peaceful country, but because it is a country that has paid such very heavy prices for war over a century and a half or even two centuries, if one includes Napoleon's invasion of Russia. And so, this view of the Soviet Union tends to see it more in terms of its history and geography than its ideology, and it tends to see less of a clear break between the Communist Revolution, now sixty years on, and the policy the Czars pursued for many centuries before that; in other words, one sees the continuities of history beginning to reemerge. Of course, that means that the Soviet Union is excessively worried about external threats, but that its occasionally neurotic and extreme behavior, including the massive buildup of its defense forces over recent years, may be more due to fear than to any intention to launch a major invasion of the West or of Western Europe in particular, though one might indeed see such an invasion for reasons concerned with preemptive strikes.

AN IDEAL THAT FAILED

The second great question is the extent to which the Soviet Union poses a threat to the West in its ideological shape as distinct from its geographical and historic importance as the major power apart from the United States in the world at the present time. In other words, what challenge does the Soviet Union's political and economic system now present to our democracies? There isn't any doubt that at its birth and for some years afterwards, Communism presented an extremely exciting and attractive ideology to many individuals in the Western democracies. Please note that I am distinguishing here between the Western democracies and the nations of the Third World, where I believe the impact to be very different. So it is with the Western democracies that I will concern myself for the next few moments. The great attraction of Communism is that it attempted to realize within this world an ideal which, as one reads Marx, is not so very far from the Augustinian concept of the City of God on earth. The idea of the state withering away, and the idea of a society without class or exploitation or conflict, is simply a Messianic vision and not a secular political vision.

The sad thing, of course, about the Communist ideal and the Communist challenge is that Communism has got stuck: it has never got beyond the second stage, that is to say, the Marxist dictatorship of the proletariat, to the third stage where the proletariat itself begins to abandon its control because of the withering away of the state and its instruments of control. In a strange way, Marx became a Messianic Jew in the later part of his theory, though not so much in the earlier parts. It is very significant, because this was the implicit goal and ideal of the Communist Revolution. Why then has it got stuck? It got stuck, I would suggest, essentially on the point Lord Acton remarked in his famous and still valid comment that power tends to corrupt, and absolute power corrupts absolutely. The class that came to power—never quite the proletariat, but those who claimed to speak in its name—became indeed, a new and powerful bureaucracy. They were, of course, the cadres of the Communist Party. They could not be overthrown or challenged; their power was monolithic and complete. And what has happened over the last sixty years is that increasingly they have become a uniquely privileged class. The *nomenclatura,* the body from which the senior Communist officials are drawn, is already more privileged than those around them. They have privileged access to housing and cars, to shops and consumer goods which are simply no longer available to the population as a whole. In short, the new class has come more and more to resemble the old class.

Not so very long ago I went to the Soviet Union and traveled with an ambassador from a Third World country that the Soviet Union at the time was doing its best to woo. As a result, he was often given access to a car normally used only by the most important people in the Soviet hierarchy. I was astonished to see as we drove up to one of the ancient Orthodox cathedrals in Moscow that the old people crossed themselves as they moved back from the car. It reminded me of nothing so much as that great scene in *Boris Gudunov* after the coronation of the son. And so, again and again, what one sees is that much of the challenge of an originally radical and idealistic movement has, in fact, been transformed into something quite conservative—a gerontocracy that finds it extremely difficult to share or decentralize its power and that is deeply suspicious of its own members on the question of succession, as the speculations about Mr. Brezhnev's successor made clear. In short, the Soviet Union has become in many ways a cautious country, an elderly country, and one that is showing signs of increasing generational stress.

The economy, too, is changing, and changing in very interesting ways. As the Soviet economy and the economies of Eastern Europe stagger under the burden of a defense budget they cannot seem to contain, as they face up to the almost unmitigated disaster of collectivization in agriculture, slowly the Communist economic system is beginning to change, despite its past rigidity and inflexibility. For unless it changes, the Soviet Bloc will have great difficulty in meeting the expectations of its own people. And so, what one is beginning to see is a fascinating evolution—a Communist economy that is slowly accepting private holdings in agriculture, indeed, actually selling back collectivized land to private ownership in countries like Hungary and Czechoslovakia; a Communist economy, in the case of Hungary, which is gradually changing into a mixed economy as small private businesses are allowed to start up and as craftsmen are allowed to sell their wares outside the official market structures; and an economy which, like our own, is increasingly developing a parallel, unofficial economy, quite apart from the formal administrative structure. Indeed, I would be so bold as to say (though it will be some years before you know whether I'm right or wrong) that, barring a major war, it is very probable that by the year 2000 the economy of the Soviet Bloc and the economy of the West will look much more like one another then we believe possible today. In many ways, this transformation of the Communist economy represents one of the most significant alterations in the balance of our world order and could ultimately lead to a meeting of minds and philosophies that we find very difficult today to comprehend.

What has precipitated the breakup of this highly monolithic structure is not a change of principles but the sharp prod of necessity. Where that necessity is least blunted by ideology, which is, of course, in the Communist Parties of Western Europe, the change is even faster. It is worth pointing out that, as recently as 1980, the Communist Parties of Spain, Yugoslavia and Italy refused to take any part in the Communist Conference of that year as a protest against the invasion of Afghanistan by the Soviet Union. It is already well known that the Italian and Spanish Communist Parties have distanced themselves from the doctrine of the dictatorship of the proletariat, declaring that in their view it no longer applies. In both cases these two Communist Parties have embraced pluralism in politics and have explicitly defined that term as accepting the possibility that a Communist government might be succeeded by a non-Communist government that would undo its reforms. In short, Eurocommunism too shows signs of a painful but quite rapid evolution.

It is crucial for us to remember the reason for this. In the years since the end of the Second World War, the supreme achievement of the West has been to offer to the average man and woman a measure of freedom and an improvement in their standard of living that the Communist regimes have not in any way been able to parallel. It is, I believe, this economic and political achievement—the fact that we have been able to combine political liberty, at least within our own territories, with economic prosperity, the diminution of poverty and relatively full employment—that has done more than any other single thing to undermine the pretensions and the criticisms implicit in the Communist Revolution. It will not, therefore, surprise you if I go on to say that what would most put that achievement at risk in the Western democracies would be any policy that once again lent credence to the suspicion that mixed economies dominated by the private sector inevitably carry with them impoverishment, differential standards between one section of the community and another, and no opportunities for those who are impoverished or black or come from deprived sections of society. I believe that would do more to aid the Communist challenge than virtually any other single thing we might do.

THE USSR AND THE THIRD WORLD

Having made that rather controversial statement, let me turn to the third question: The impact of the Soviet Bloc and of Communism on the Third World. And here, let me say again, I believe to some extent the impact of the Soviet Union on the Third World has been exaggerated. Yes, it is important, and certainly in a military sense, the appearance of Cuban troops in Africa, the Soviet invasion of Afghanistan, the extension of Soviet interests and Soviet influence in

Latin America and elsewhere are significant and important. But it is also significant and important not to get so absorbed in this thought that one fails to notice three other things.

The first is the extraordinary capacity that Africa has to turn everything back into something which is uniquely African, to absorb all of our Western and Soviet ideologies and to make of them something quite different. The evolution of Africa has been towards a specifically African kind of polity, a single party state, but not towards permanently clear ideological divisions of the kind that many of us believed to be likely to occur as a result of the developments of the early sixties and the early seventies. The significance of China is, above all, the evidence of a split in the Communist Church which nothing whatever can put back together. The Chinese are not very likely, I believe, to get very close again to the Soviet Union, for their evolution has proven to be markedly less ideological. The Chinese are essentially a very pragmatic power, willing to work with anyone who can improve their economic and scientific prospects. There is, thirdly, and no less important for its continual neglect by the West, the vast country of India, which has consistently resisted a great deal of wooing by the Soviet Union in order to remain distinctly Indian. India insists on its own kind of democracy, its own kind of nonalignment, and it stubbornly refuses to get caught up in the ideological battles between ourselves and the Soviet Bloc. For India almost invariably takes the viewpoint that time is eternity and that, therefore, one should not get too absorbed in the immediate political worries of this year, next year, or the year after.

What this all adds up to (and obviously I would like to develop these points at greater length than I could possibly have time to do tonight), I think, is a statement from the Third World saying, "For God's sake, leave us alone. We want you to help us in ways that we lay down. We want your economic and technological knowledge. We want to be able to discuss and to negotiate and to take part in mediation with you, but we do not want to have imposed upon us your ideological battles." Moreover, I think we often don't appreciate sufficiently in the West that the Soviet Union is seen by the Third World as being part of the First World and not part of itself.

CHALLENGE TO THE WEST

Which brings me to the last part of what I want to say. Primary here is the major moral issue of what happens to the arms race and whether those of us who try to think about where we are going can indeed ultimately conceive of the idea of nuclear war. I believe that for those of the Christian and Jewish heritage this presents the most acute and difficult moral problem of all. The Social Democratic Party to which I belong has not rejected as unthinkable any use of nuclear weapons. It has, however, moved towards the point of view that everything possible must be done to limit and control and to reduce the likelihood of the use of those nuclear weapons. I suppose that one reason for this is the recognition that, at the present moment, the removal of Western Europe from the NATO alliance because of its nuclear threat might well destabilize the world in a way that made it more dangerous rather than less. But there are, I think, very difficult problems for those who think profoundly about the future of the human race in this whole area. At the moment what I would certainly say, and I'm sorry to have to use a short-term perspective, is that the Western Alliance must put more effort, more determination, and more sheer energy behind demands for arms control than has been done up to now.

I believe that the West will lose its moral position in the world if it does not give the same degree of priority to arms control and limitation that it has up to now given to defense. And I also believe, though this is a more expedient thought, that we will see a very great growth of the peace movement throughout the whole of the West if the members of the peace movement, many of whom are not in any sense fellow travelers with Communism, are not persuaded that the West is bending its best efforts to this end. It should be said in this context about President Carter that in 1977 he made on behalf of the United States administration probably the most far-reaching proposal ever made in the field of arms control. It is a matter of the most profound regret that at that time the Soviet Union neither believed him nor trusted him and eventually rejected those proposals. It takes a long time to reestablish the political prerequisites of another such move forward. And yet I believe we are now very close to the point where we ought to try to do so, for two reasons in particular. The first flows from the work of Professor Daniel Frei of Zurich University, whom some of you may know as one of the major experts now advising the UN Disarmament Commission. His work, which is based on historical and geographical models, indicates that it is much more likely that nuclear war would start from an escalation of a Third World clash—a clash, more precisely, outside the Soviet-American balance of terror—than that it would start within that balance or purely as a result of an accident. He contends that the management of nuclear arms in the West and the Soviet Bloc is more sophisticated than it used to be and that accidents are less, not more, likely than they were.

But when we look outside that immediate area, what do we see? We see a situation in the Middle East where the balance of peace and war has got terrifyingly close to tipping toward escalation, with a consequent spilling out of conflict from that desperate cockpit of the world. The Israeli attack on the Iraqi nuclear power station is just one demonstration of how close we are living to the edges of what may be desperately dangerous. In that context, I would like to say that President Reagan's Middle East peace initiative is profoundly welcome, because it recognizes the endless underlying instability of the relationship between Israel and her neighbors by trying to suggest that there must be some sort of long-term solution to the problems while there is still time. I say "while there is still time" advisedly because I think the most frightening thing about the Middle East is that it is daily becoming an increasingly armed and militaristic camp. The Iran-Iraqi war already has a tremendous casualty list, and Israel herself is becoming, willy-nilly, increasingly a military power in which military imperatives take precedence. I say that as somebody who believes very strongly that Israel suffers from the great burden of being judged by a higher standard than other countries because she herself, as her President said so eloquently two weeks ago, has chosen to be so judged. And, by that judgment, Israel at the time of the Beirut massacre, unquestionably and perhaps to some extent not wholly fairly, was held in part responsible even though she herself was not directly and at first hand involved.

The second area of the world that, I believe, presents us with grave moral problems is Poland. And, here again, for lack of time, I think I can only say this: to my mind one of the most acute problems that faces us in the NATO alliance is how far we can argue morally that we should make financial credits available without condition and on more generous terms than we do to the Third World, to countries of the Soviet Bloc, or for that matter to countries outside the Soviet Bloc, that have uniquely damaged the most essential human rights. A week ago in London I met one of the philosophers of the Solidarity Movement. His name is Dr. Lipski and he is one of the great thinkers behind Solidarity. He is clear, as Solidarity itself is clear, that the thrust of the movement goes to the very heart of Marxism-Leninism because it questions the monolithic structure of the dictatorship of the Party over the State, what we now know to be the operative version of the dictatorship of the proletariat. Dr. Lipski has gone back to Poland. He'd been in Britain to have an operation on his heart, and I asked him why he was returning since it was clear that he was going back to certain arrest—as has indeed happened. His reply was one that those of us who are concerned about Poland must bear in mind. He said, "I have to show the workers that intellectuals also have some courage." It was a remarkable statement by a very brave man. He also said that he believed that the United States was right in thinking that there should be some conditions attached to the refinancing of the Polish debt, not as a general proposition but as a specific proposition in a specific case where we all know the West will not and cannot militarily intervene.

BEYOND NATIONALISM

And so, finally, two concluding thoughts. The first one is this: I have said already that I believe that the greatest single danger for the West is also its greatest single hope: that the West must be able to continue to demonstrate that in libertarian mixed economies the issues thought by Communists, and by many citizens of the Soviet Bloc, to be only resolvable in Communist terms, have been indeed more satisfactorily solved within our own countries. In short, the social and economic achievements of the West, not least the achievement of social justice, of relatively full employment, are absolutely crucial to the whole moral position that we adopt. In the end, to adopt Khruschev's phrase, we will bury Communism by simply proving that the Western Democratic approach is better for the ordinary man and woman in the street. That, of course, raises the question of our attitude towards tolerance between the races, tolerance between the sexes, because that is what we will be judged by, and so we should be.

And then, beyond that, there lies another question, a question on which I shall end: Can we go on very much longer believing that a world which is confronted by problems that are at the very least supranational can be dealt with by institutions that remain obstinately national? The Atlantic Alliance, the Soviet Bloc itself, the European Community, are all infant and primitive steps towards some kind of authority that lies beyond the nation state. The nation state, even the nation state as big as the United States or the Soviet Union, clearly cannot any longer deal effectively with some of the most crucial problems of our age. Nation states cannot deal effectively with environmental pollution: the smoke of Pittsburgh eventually ends in the forests of Sweden. Nor can they deal effectively with peace; we have not yet got anything more than a series of ad hoc measures for trying to establish peace, the most recent example being the sudden creation of a multinational force to go out to the Lebanon, its quick recall and its equally quick return. Time and again we desperately fall back upon just this kind of temporary expedient.

It is evident that we have not yet got any supranational answers, as the next lecture in this series will further indicate when it explores the growing gap between the Third World and the First World and, as part of that, the danger of collapse in the world financial and economic system posed by the reneging of a major Third World country on its debts. We are, in short, living from hand to mouth in a situation where the institutions established after the Second World War (General Agreements on Tariffs and Trade, the International Monetary Fund, the United Nations itself) are becoming obsolete. What we need most of all, therefore, is the political vision and imagination to begin to develop institutions that are capable of dealing with the problems of our world. And we also need to start saying out loud that there is a perilous lack of symmetry between the political institutions that we have created (good as they have been) and the problems that we are now confronting and have to deal with over the next few decades.

Discussion

Q: If the Socialist Democratic Party were to come to power in a coalition or on its own, could you give me some idea how it would differ specifically from the present Conservative government in its relations with the Soviet Union?

A: Yes, one of the first things that we would do would be to press for the cancellation of Trident, and I think that we would almost certainly make this a condition of entering into a coalition with any other major party. We believe that Trident represents a disturbing escalation of the arms race by those countries outside the major blocs that possess nuclear weapons, and we fear that they may cause a considerable disturbance in the arms control discussions now going ahead, because, as you will be aware, neither the British nor the French deterrents are involved in those negotiations, and Trident, of course, will make the British deterrent a very much larger one than it is at the present time. I use the term "British deterrent" as shorthand, of course, for at the present time it is under the control of NATO, but the Trident would be built by Britain and would be an addition to the British force and not specifically to the NATO forces. That is the first position.

Our second position, still in that same field, is that we are increasingly, as a party, pressing for the idea of a nuclear-free area on both sides of the border between Western and Eastern Europe, or, if you like, along the Iron Curtain. That isn't the same thing, incidentally, as the proposal for a nuclear-free zone. It is the idea of restricting or indeed eliminating the use of nuclear weapons by having a sort of *cordon sanitaire* on either side of the Iron Curtain; it is, incidentally, the idea that was put forward by the Common Security Commission in its recent presentation to the United Nations and elsewhere.

Thirdly, with respect to relations with the Soviet Union, I've indicated that we would be rather more ready (I can't put it any more strongly than that) to consider whether there are certain cases where some economic sanctions would be sensible. In the case of the pipeline, I fear that a good American case was lost because it was brought forward far too late, long after the contracts were signed, and in a situation where I don't think any European government could very easily propose that those contracts should be gone back on. But the American position which was originally advanced, namely, the dangerous degree of energy dependence by Europe on the Soviet Bloc, has some validity, as does the position that the United States raised about attaching conditions to any rescheduling of the Polish debt. Incidentally, there is one other point that I should make very broadly: as you probably know, we are a strongly pro-EEC party and would therefore wish to see an evolution of the European community— for example, the acceptance of a common electoral system for elections to the European Parliament, which is beyond any position the old parties in Britain share.

Q: Mrs. Williams, you spoke about the desirability of having an effective international organization. Almost forty years ago, idealists set about organizing such an organization in the United Nations and that, of course, has not worked out. I'm wondering how you envisage that the type of body you speak of would be formed and how those efforts would differ from the ones made in connection with the formation of the United Nations?

A: I think I would say that one of the great drawbacks of idealists is that they often don't appreciate that practice is always going to fall short of their ideals. Let me answer your question by asking another one: Would the world be better off today if we didn't have the United Nations? I think the answer to that, at least for me, is very clearly, No, it would not be better off. While I do agree with you that in many ways the United Nations has clearly fallen short of the ideals of its founders, it has also been an extremely important safety valve for many of the conflicts in the world. The fact that it has been possible to bring problems to the United Nations and even to some extent to achieve a certain amount of international agreement, particularly in relation to certain of the conflicts in the Third World, is of very great importance. I also believe it has served a valuable function as a platform for many Third World countries. So, rather than say, Shouldn't we start all over again? I would rather propose that we evolve from what we have; and that means, among other things, that I myself would like to see an attempt again to reestablish the concept of, if not a permanent standing police force, at least a truly international peace-keeping force that could be called up at very short notice indeed—subject, of course, to the decision of the Security Council or in certain cases, of the General Assembly. I believe, in other words, that we've got to move towards the concept of a standing international police force, in however elementary a form, which could be used for certain purposes, particularly to stop the escalation of what are sometimes called fire-brigade situations. I personally would go further than that and hope that one day there will be an acceptance of a greater degree of world authority, greater than anything we've seen yet in the United Nations; but I believe that to be a long way off.

Q: You outlined two broad views of the nature of the Soviet system. Very briefly, you indicated one view sees the Soviet system as inherently aggressive, determined to export revolution and to destroy the freedoms of the free world, and you summarized it rather radically as anti-Christ. The other view is that the Soviets are neurotically defensive and suspicious and that they fear war and so forth and so on. These generally align well with arguments pursued by those who fear that United States foreign policy might be predicated on an anti-Communist posture. Which of those views does your Party or yourself adhere to, because whatever decisions on foreign policy your Party might make, they ultimately would have to be predicated upon some coherent view of the nature of the Soviet system. It is not clear to me which of those two views you would support or, to put the matter very briefly, would you endorse and support a foreign policy predicated on an anti-Communist crusade, as I'm sure you would support a foreign policy predicated on an anti-Fascist crusade?

A: No, I wouldn't, and I think it must be rather clear why. I believe that a foreign policy predicated on an anti-Communist crusade will hand a very large part of the world over to the interests of the Soviet Bloc, because I think the danger of an anti-Communist crusade is that it treats those who are not with us as if they are against us; moreover, it tends to erect a structure of far right to oppose far left, and that in my view is where the whole thing goes desperately wrong. I think what I'm suggesting is that the West's greatest strength in being opposed or in standing against Communism (I am certainly very anti-Communist) lies in the West's ability to put before the peoples of the world a social and economic program which is far more attractive than that of Communism. I think that Communism essentially has begun to destroy itself, and I think that by treating the appeal of Communism as if it were still as strong as it once used to be, we will, in fact, weaken our own position very seriously indeed. So, yes, if the West is true to its ideals, and if it pursues the extraordinarily successful policies that it has pursued over the last twenty years, I have no fear at all about the outcome, and I believe that it can be achieved without war.

Q: You have not answered my question. Which of those two views that you outlined do you subscribe to? That the Soviet Union is aggressive and destructive?

A: Sorry, I think the second. I think the Soviet Union is not a naturally aggressive power; I think it is a neurotically defensive power, but I think that being neurotically defensive means that it will take every advantage it can. The distinction that I'm trying to make is between the Soviet Union and Nazi Germany, which would take advantage and then, at a certain point, cease to make any realistic judgment at all, because it became convinced that its role in the world was to destroy everything that was not itself Nazism. I do not believe the Soviet Union is like this. I believe the Soviet Union, in the end, is a relatively pragmatic power that will never pursue its ideals (if you would like to call them that) at the risk of a major world war. I think if there is going to be a major world war it will come in the ways that I have described and not by the deliberate choice of the Soviet Union or, for that matter, of the United States.

Q: It has been widely suggested that a rather significant political and ideological gap has emerged between the United States and the European Community. My question is how significant do you think that gap is and what can be done to rectify the situation?

A: I think it is quite a significant gap. I think that part of it is inevitable, that is to say, that as the European Community begins to develop its own common political approaches—and its has begun to do that, as for example, over the Middle East at the United Nations—you are going to see for the first time considerable differences of emphasis and even sometimes a difference of viewpoint. Now that has emerged already, and I wouldn't worry too much about it. You cannot see any development of the European Community without there being some divergence between the United States and Europe. But I think there have been three recent developments that go much beyond this organic dislocation that is inevitable. First of all, the question of the pipeline. I briefly referred to that. I think the United States had a strong case that was largely wrecked by the timetable, because the United States did not raise the issue until after General Haig had left the State Department, possibly because, as he said recently, he was against sanctions on the pipeline and therefore when it came forward as an issue, it was already impossibly late. I also think that, to some extent, the American position was made difficult by the United States's own decision to renew the grain agreement with the Soviet Union. There are many arguments, of course, that the grain agreement is quite different from the pipeline, but in simple political terms people just say that the United States doesn't mind doing trade with Russia, it just objects to *your* doing trade with Russia. It is a very easy argument to make.

On the second issue—about Poland—there has again been a rift about the extent to which the West should react to the establishment of the Polish military government and the way it has behaved since it has been established. You will have perceived from my remarks that I personally have some sympathy for the American view on that and some sympathy with the view that it is a bit much, in the light of all that has happened, to see Western banks lending very, very large sums of money to Poland on a more favorable basis than they do to Third World countries. Thus, I have considerable sympathy with the U.S. view that there ought to be rather more reaction than there has been so far to the situation in Poland. On the question of arms, I can only say very briefly that it is going to be extremely difficult having the cruise missiles installed in Western Europe; but, on the other hand, Western Europe ought to remember that the original request came not from the United States but from Western Europe itself. Therefore, if Western Europe takes the view that the installation of these missiles is going to be politically very difficult (and I haven't any doubt about it), not least in Germany at the present time, then I think it is for Western Europeans to reconsider what the position ought to be and to come up with fresh proposals. Let me add one other thing which I think is worth saying. I think that the meeting the day before yesterday of the NATO foreign ministers in Quebec is the kind of thing that ought to happen on a much more regular basis within the Alliance. It seems to me a great mistake that such meetings are only held very rarely by heads of state and that there is no regular mechanism for hammering out the political aspects of the Alliance. It is treated far too often merely as a military alliance, and I don't think it can be treated that way very much longer.

Q: Given over twenty million unemployed in the United States and Western Europe, and the resulting pressures on government to reduce spending on social programs, what do you think of the prospects for maintaining that moral superiority that you say is the real strength of the Western democracies?

A: I think at the moment the prospects are rather poor. I think that dealing with the problem of unemployment is an absolutely essential moral and economic issue that we have to direct ourselves to. I don't believe we can afford to see a permanent underclass being created in all of our countries, mostly in the cities, mostly among the deprived, and sometimes among blacks, and simply write off this section of society. We are getting dangerously close to that point both in my country and in your own.

You are now going to say, "What do we do about it?" and I was about to say that I would like to lecture for about another hour on that, but I will just give you two examples. I think that one of the great areas where we could indeed employ far more people is in the renewal of a rapidly deteriorating infrastructure, both in the United States and in my own country. Much of it was built in the nineteenth century; I mean the system of older housing, the inner city environment, sewage and drainage facilities, and so forth. This is an area that is labor-intensive and where I believe we will see or ought to see real opportunities for genuine employment and not mere make-work.

The second great area of this kind, I believe, lies in recognizing that we are likely in the long run to see increasing energy costs. Thus, another huge area of employment opportunity lies in the whole area of switching from energy inefficient processes, upon which much of our two economies are based, to much more energy-efficient procedures. Whether we think here of the conservation of energy in housing or the character of our transport systems or the nature of our industrial processes, there is a huge opportunity to create far more jobs than we dream possible at the present time. I think it is the political will that is missing more than any other single thing, and I believe, though I don't have time to go into it now, that there are ways of dealing with inflationary pressures that we aren't at the moment prepared to face up to.

Q: What consequences do you expect from the fall of Chancellor Schmidt's government in West Germany?

A: I don't think there will be a great many consequences from the fall of Chancellor Schmidt. His government was in power for so long that I think for the last year and a half people have been forecasting the possibility or even probability that the Social Democratic Government would fall. Let me say, however, that I think Herr Schmidt has probably been our most remarkable postwar statesman or at least one of the most remarkable, putting to one side wartime leaders like Churchill and Roosevelt and so on. I think that in peacetime he has been possibly the most outstanding statesman in the West, and I believe we all owe him a very great deal. I think, however, that West German policy is likely to be relatively continuous, with one great caveat by way of a footnote to that: if the Greens (the Environmental Party) do replace the Free Democrats as the crucial hinge party which determines in state after state, as it now does in Hamburg, the shape of the government, then I think we are going to go through a rather unstable period because, of course, the Greens fundamentally do not believe in government. They are to a great extent philosophically anarchistic, and therefore I've taken the view that they cannot take responsibility for making decisions of government. That could give rise to quite a serious and difficult problem, so I don't take quite so complacent a view as I've certainly heard in some quarters in the United States. Such a changeover would not be quite so easy as is sometimes now supposed.

DENIS GOULET

The Relationship between Rich Nations and Poor

Denis Goulet is O'Neill Professor of Education at the University of Notre Dame, a noted expert in the field of development, and author of *The Cruel Choice*. This lecture was given on October 18, 1982.

MEANS AND ENDS IN DEVELOPMENT

High unemployment has brought itinerant hoboes back to the American scene. Like their Depression counterparts, today's vagrants hop freight trains, sleep in empty lots, and live by their wits. *The Hobo News*, that classic newspaper of yesteryear, was fond of citing the clever adage: "Give me enough luxuries and I'll do without the necessities." In the real world, however, as Lewis Mumford wrote in 1934:

> Genuine value lies in the power to sustain or enrich life . . . the juice of a lemon may be more valuable on a long ocean voyage than a hundred pounds of meat without it.[1]

Like Mumford, thoughtful economists have always gone beyond the calculus of instrumental means: they are concerned with ends. Let me introduce this evening's ethical reflection on obstacles to world development by citing a few such economists.

Exhibit A is Richard Tawney (1880-1962), author of such diverse works as *Religion and the Rise of Capitalism, English Economic History,* and *Land and Labour in China*. In his 1920 study *The Acquisitive Society*, Tawney complained that:

> Industrial communities neglect the very objects for which it is worthwhile to acquire riches in their feverish preoccupation with the means by which riches can be acquired.[2]

For John Kenneth Galbraith, writing forty-two years later,

> The final requirement of modern development planning is that it have a theory of consumption . . . a view of what the production is ultimately for.[3]

Galbraith had graced the frontispiece of his earlier best-selling work, *The Affluent Society,* with a phrase drawn from Alfred Marshall: "The economist, like everyone else, must concern himself with the ultimate aims of man."[4] Finally, Adolf Berle noted in the early 1950s:

---

1. Lewis Mumford, *Technics and Civilization* (New York: Harcourt, Brace, 1934), p. 76.
2. Cited in John Bartlett, *Familiar Quotations,* 15th ed. (Boston: Little, Brown, 1980), p. 773.
3. John Kenneth Galbraith, *Economic Development in Perspective* (Cambridge: Harvard University Press, 1962), p. 43.
4. John Kenneth Galbraith, *The Affluent Society* (Boston: Houghton Mifflin, 1958).

that the really great corporation managements have reached a position for the first time in their history in which they must consciously take account of philosophical considerations . . . they must consider at least in its more elementary phases the ancient problem of the "good life."[5]

Economists, accordingly, must take it as part of their mission to clarify how goods can help people reach the good life.[6] Such teleological reflection is not a luxury to be indulged in by a few philosophically inclined specialists, however: it is the urgent duty of all citizens responsible for the stewardship of our planet. Speaking for the North-South Commission which he chaired, Willy Brandt calls development a life-and-death issue for humanity at large.[7] Although many observers decry the scandal of mass poverty in the world, the real scandal is not widespread poverty, but the coexistence of outrageously wasteful wealth alongside degrading misery. It is shocking that a few human beings possess far more than they need in order to be fully human, while most others lack enough to live a human life.

Why have privileged nations and social classes, even when they profess moral ideals of compassion and justice, failed to mount a successful war on global poverty? Perhaps the answer lies in the tragic nature of history itself.[8] In his provocative *Reflections on the Causes of Human Misery,* the Harvard historian Barrington Moore argues that deliberate attempts to improve the human condition have themselves been a major cause of misery throughout history, one that is no less destructive than the selfish neglect of others' sufferings.[9]

If Moore is right, the ultimate ethical question in development is whether or not it is futile to strive to improve the lot of 800 million human beings. These are the people who live in "absolute poverty," a condition of life, according to Robert McNamara,

---

5. Adolf A. Berle, Jr., *The 20th Century Capitalist Revolution* (New York: Harcourt, Brace, 1954), p. 166.
6. On this, see Denis Goulet, "Sufficiency for All: The Basic Mandate of Development and Social Economics," *Review of Social Economy* 36:3 (December 1978), pp. 243-61.
7. Willy Brandt, "Introduction" to *North-South, A Program for Survival,* ed. Anthony Sampson (Cambridge: MIT Press, 1980), pp. 7, 13, and 29.
8. On this, see Jean-Marie Domenach, *Le Retour du Tragique* (Paris: Editions du Seuil, 1963).
9. Barrington Moore, Jr., *Reflections on the Causes of Human Misery* (Boston: Beacon Press, 1970).

so characterized by malnutrition, illiteracy, disease, squalid surroundings, high infant mortality, and low life expectancy as to
be beneath any reasonable definition of human decency.[10]

Policy "realists" invoke historical fatalism to justify their inaction or
timid palliative solutions in the face of global poverty. It is more constructive, they argue, or at least safer, to preserve existing social
orders than to experiment with new arrangements in vain hopes of
constructing better systems. There is, admittedly, some semblance of
truth to their claim that efforts to build new systems often lead to
worse disorders.[11] No magic buttons can be pressed or Utopian
wands waved which will make institutions serve the poor. Yet can
any morality exist unless human actors resist the paralysis induced by
too "objective" a view of the difficulties lying in the way of structural change? Has not human nobility always consisted in reversing
all odds? Moral agendas are predicated, not on accepting things as
they are, but on striving to make them what they ought to be. To
create new possibilities is the supreme moral imperative, in the arena
of global poverty as in that of disarmament.

Two opposite readings of the dictum "Politics is the art of the
possible" vie for legitimacy. One exegesis sees the political art as
wheeling and dealing within closed boundaries of possibility, what
Lyndon Johnson called "horse trading." If political practitioners
assume that boundaries of possibility are given once and for all, they
will strive to maximize particular gains within closed boundaries. Inevitably, this approach becomes conservative, dedicated to system
maintenance. A contrary exegesis defines politics as the art of
creating new possibilities. Frontiers of possibility must be expanded
both by implosion (pushing the system's limits outwards through
pressure from within) and by explosion (rupturing continuities
through outside forces pressing in). Reformists, revolutionaries, and
progressives favor this second exegesis.

By its very nature, development politics must aim at creating
new possibilities. The very internal exigencies of development call
for new structures, new institutions, new criteria for problem solving, and new ground rules to govern relations between rich and poor,
within national borders as beyond them. Therefore, the stewards of
present global circulation systems cannot be the architects of genuine

---

10. Robert S. McNamara, "Foreword" to *World Development Report, 1978*
    (Washington, D.C.: World Bank, 1978), p. iii.
11. For more on this, see Denis Goulet, "Is Economic Justice Possible?"
    Cross Currents 31:1 (Spring 1981), pp. 35-51.

development. Even so temperate an observer as Gunnar Myrdal explains why:

> The theory of international trade was not worked out to explain the reality of underdevelopment and the need for development. One might say, rather, that this imposing structure of abstract reasoning implicitly had almost the opposite purpose, that of *explaining away the international equality problem.*[12]

This agonistic vision of the ethical task summons us to find leverage points for triumphing over the major obstacles impeding sound development. Accordingly, three such obstacles will now be analyzed: (1) the bankruptcy of development paradigms, (2) the global paralysis of institutional imagination, and (3) domestic impediments to sound Third World development. Afterwards, and in conclusion, I shall evoke the general posture ethics must adopt in promoting the four dimensions of authentic development.

BANKRUPTCY OF DEVELOPMENT PARADIGMS

Denouncing mainstream development models is merely "bringing coals to Newcastle": experts themselves now charge conventional paradigms with bankruptcy. Indeed, the very champions of earlier development strategies search, at times with frantic urgency, for alternatives.[13] These are needed because earlier prescriptions failed in four domains: distribution, employment, self-reliance, and human costs.

1. Distribution. Conventional strategies have not led to satisfactory economic growth in most Third World countries. The world's thirty-six poorest countries averaged GNP growth rates, between 1960 and 1979, of 1.6 percent, while at the same time undergoing a population increase of 2.1 percent yearly.[14] And even where high growth did occur, it generated massive inequities in the distribu-

---

12. Gunnar Myrdal, *The Challenge of World Poverty* (New York: Pantheon, 1970), p. 277. Italics are Myrdal's.
13. See *What Now? Another Development* (Uppsala, Sweden: Dag Hammarskjold Foundation, 1975); cf. Marc Nerfin, ed., *Another Development: Approaches and Strategies* (Uppsala, Sweden: Dag Hammarskjold Foundation, 1977).
14. World Bank, *World Bank Development Report 1981* (Washington, D.C.: World Bank, 1981), pp. 134 and 166.

tion of benefits among people of diverse classes, regions, and nations. General Emilio Garrastazu-Medici, Brazil's president from 1969 to 1974, was once asked by a journalist what he thought of the "economic miracle," a reference to Brazil's GNP growth rates of over 10 percent yearly between 1967 and 1971. With unaccustomed candor, Medici replied: "The miracle is good for Brazil's economy, but bad for its people." Studies commissioned by Brazil's national conference of bishops reveal that

> The average income of the 5 percent of the richest individuals in 1970 was almost seventeen times greater than that of the 50 percent of the poorest population. By 1976 it was thirty-three times larger.[15]

One is surely entitled to ask: What kind of development is good for an abstraction known as the national economy, but bad for the flesh-and-blood people that economy is meant to serve?

Inequitable distribution of growth's benefits widens existing disparities because small percentage gains in income for the already rich add absolute increments to their income far greater than those accruing even to high percentage increases for the poor. Most researchers studying distribution measure differences in income and in access to basic social services such as health care, pure water, minimal housing and schooling, and inexpensive public transportation to work and marketplace.[16] Few studies are conducted, however, to gauge differences in accumulated wealth and assets, clearly a more enduring source of disparities between rich and poor.

2. Employment. Strategies prescribing industrial growth and high technology also failed to create jobs. Numerous ILO (International Labor Office) studies show that rapid industrialization and growth in GNP do not reduce unemployment.[17] One such study notes

---

15. Cited in René Dumont and Marie-France Mottin, *Le Mal-Développement en Amérique Latine* (Paris: Editions du Seuil, 1981).
16. Morris David Morris, *Measuring the Condition of the World's Poor: The Physical Quality of Life Index* (New York: Pergamon, 1979); cf. Roger D. Hansen et al., *U.S. Foreign Policy and the Third World, Agenda 1982* (New York: Praeger, 1982), Statistical Indices, pp. 129-246.
17. See International Labor Office (ILO), *Towards full employment: A programme for Colombia, prepared by an interagency team organised by the International Labour Office* (Geneva, 1970); ILO, *Matching employment opportunities and expectations: A programme of action for Ceylon,* report and technical papers in 2 vols. (Geneva, 1971); ILO,

cryptically that "The tragic waste of human resources in the Third World is symbolized by nearly 300 million persons unemployed or underemployed in the mid-1970s."[18] Modern industrial investments are too expensive to create enough workplaces for large numbers of unskilled workers. By definition, however, the labor force of Third World countries is composed mainly of such unskilled workers. Or, to speak more accurately, their skills are those of subsistence food growers and artisans. Hence a policy aimed at mechanizing agricultural production exacerbates the problem: it displaces peasants from their livelihood without providing them with new sources of productive work and income. The World Bank describes the mechanisms at work in these terms:

> Because average labor productivity is lower in agriculture than in industry or services, the sectoral restructuring of the labor force initially proceeds more slowly than that of production. As a result, agriculture so far remains the predominant source of employment not only in Low Income countries but also in many Middle Income countries.

> The larger number of workers remaining in agriculture in developing countries has increasingly raised doubts about the adequacy of the industrialization process as a source of remunerative employment.[19]

Gandhi made a vital distinction when he preached the superiority of production by the masses over mass production. The first brings jobs and dignity to large numbers of poor village people unfamiliar with new technologies; the second renders their labor and skills superfluous by concentrating production in large, urban factory units

---

Employment, incomes and inequality: A strategy for increasing productive employment in Kenya (Geneva, 1972); ILO, *Employment and income policies for Iran* (Geneva, 1973); ILO, *Sharing in development: A programme of employment, equity and growth for the Philippines* (Geneva, 1974); ILO, *Generación de empleo productivo y crecimiento económico: el caso de la República Dominicana* (Geneva, 1975); ILO, *Growth, employment and equity: A comprehensive strategy for Sudan* (Geneva, 1976) (provisional edition).

18. See ILO, *Employment, Growth and Basic Needs: A One-World Problem,* "Introduction" by James P. Grant (New York: Praeger, 1977), p. 3.

19. World Bank, *World Development Report, 1979* (Washington, D.C.: World Bank, 1979), p. 46.

requiring costly imported raw materials and intermediate components.

Moreover, few Third World countries have provided incentives capable of retaining their skilled professional workers. The result is the brain drain, a disastrous hemorrhage of a poor nation's trained personnel to greener pastures in rich countries. Another distortion traceable to conventional industrialization models is the overconcentration of facilities, equipment, and job opportunities in a few large cities. The results are widespread pauperization and unemployment in the countryside, and parasitical overpopulation in cities unable to supply jobs and basic services to millions fleeing rural misery.

3. Self-Reliant Growth. Earlier development writers saw self-sustaining growth as an important criterion of progress. Walt Rostow, grandfather of the linear "stages of growth" model, assumed that, with rational resource planning and adequate levels of capital investment,

> In a decade or two both the basic structure of the economy and the social and political structure of the society are transformed in such a way that a steady rate of growth can be, thereafter, regularly sustained.[20]

Few Third World countries have achieved self-sustaining economic growth. On the contrary, most depend on recurring infusions of foreign capital and technology, at times also of food, fuels, and trained people. Astronomical debts incurred by Brazil, Mexico, and other growing countries testify to the failure of growth strategies to lessen dependency on outside resources, in this case, expensive financial capital. Conventional prescriptions did not increase dependence by accident, however. Dependency writers such as Cardoso, Amin, Gunder-Frank, and Sunkel are correct to view dependency as a necessary outcome of the very relationships binding rich to poor nations. Global interdependence is rarely horizontal, mutual, or reciprocal. Almost always it is vertical, paternalistic, and exploitative. Nevertheless, the interdependence of horse and rider is qualitatively different from that of two oarsmen rowing one boat.[21]

---

20. Walter W. Rostow, *The Stages of Economic Growth* (New York: Cambridge University Press, 1960), pp. 8-9.
21. On this, see Denis Goulet, *World Interdependence: Verbal Smokescreen or New Ethic?* Overseas Development Council Development Paper (New York: Praeger, March 1976).

If national self-reliance has proven to be an elusive goal in development history, so has self-reliance at the local level. Centralized patterns of problem solving and resource allocation reinforce biases in favor of building a few large hospitals instead of providing basic health services to everyone, of running a few prestigious schools for the elite rather than giving practical education to all, of manufacturing luxury cars for the privileged instead of inexpensive buses for the poor.[22] These counterdevelopmental paradoxes are brilliantly denounced by Ivan Illich, J.P. Naik, and other critical writers.[23] Theories of self-reliance doubtless inspired Julius Nyerere's *ujaama* philosophy and Mao Tse-Tung's Great Leap Forward, but in practice self-reliance has usually been crushed or ignored.[24] Third World countries find it difficult to conquer self-reliance because a sequence of dependency operates behind resource transfers. In early periods of development, poor countries need foreign capital, technology, managerial skills, and markets.[25] Over time, and as they reduce their dependency on foreign capital, they continue to depend on outside inputs of technology, managerial expertise, and market access. This sequence of dependency extends over long periods, keeping even relatively successful nations like South Korea or Singapore vulnerable to global market forces beyond their control.

Cultural subordination, no less than economic, political, and technological dependence, continues to plague Third World countries. Under the steamroller effects of foreign influences, their vulnerable cultures are rapidly being destroyed or badly damaged. This fate has befallen Andalusian Gypsies on the point of irrevocably forgetting their *canto-hondo* music, and primitive artists in Haiti being swept up by the demands of commercial tourism.[26] Throughout

---

22. On this, see Michael Lipton, *Why Poor People Stay Poor, Urban Bias in World Development* (Cambridge: Harvard University Press, 1976).
23. Ivan Illich, *Toward a History of Needs* (New York: Pantheon, 1978); J.P. Naik, *Some Perspectives on Non-Formal Education* (Bombay: Allied Publishers Private Ltd., 1977) and *An Alternative System of Health Care Service in India: Some Proposals* (Bombay: Allied Publishers Private, 1977).
24. Johan Galtung, Peter O'Brien, and Roy Preiswerk, eds., *Self-Reliance, A Strategy for Development* (London: Bogle-L'Ourverture Publications, 1980).
25. Denis Goulet, *The Uncertain Promise, Value Conflicts in Technology Transfer* (New York: IDOC, 1977), pp. 38-9.
26. For a study of the destruction of the artisans' way of life in the Andes, see Mirko Lauer, *Introducción a la pintura peruana del siglo XX* (Lima: Mosca Azul Editores, 1976).

the world, as Illich observes, technical values are displacing vernacular or nonelite values.[27]

4. Human Costs. Standard development paradigms have failed in yet another domain: they have exacted intolerably high costs in human suffering and cultural destruction. Sociologist Peter Berger, author of *Pyramids of Sacrifice,* counsels development planners to make a "calculus of pain" and a "calculus of meaning" before deciding how beneficial or harmful to people are their prescriptions.[28] Similarly, development novelists[29] narrate how development brings "progress" but, in the process, destroys precious values and imposes cruel sufferings upon people.[30] What goes by the name of "development" shatters family bonds and undermines cultural meaning and identity systems. Policy makers, therefore, need to design change strategies which reduce human costs to tolerable levels.[31]

Third World communities in growing numbers now raise their voices against the damage inflicted upon them in the name of development. One example of successful action taken to counter the harm wrought by "development" is offered by the fishing village of Kuala Juru in northwestern Malaysia. Villagers turned down government subsidies to move inland to factory work in the Free Trade Zone of Prai, preferring instead to remain in Kuala Juru and continue living as an "amphibious people" having the sea as their rice bowl. The government's policy of granting licenses to modern trawlers equipped with motors, sonar, and electronic nets had rapidly led to the depletion of Kuala Juru's traditional fishing beds. To make matters worse, local waters were badly polluted by the practice of dumping factory wastes offshore. The villagers reacted and decided to remain in Kuala Juru and live from the sea. They had seen the cultural

---

27. Ivan Illich, *Shadow Work* (Salem, N.H.: Marion Boyars, 1981), Ch. 2, pp. 27-52.
28. Peter L, Berger, *Pyramids of Sacrifice* (New York: Basic Books, 1974), Chapters 5 and 6.
29. For example, Chinua Achebe, *Things Fall Apart* (New York: Fawcett Crest, 1959); Cheikh Hamidou Kane, *Ambiguous Adventure* (London: Heinemann, 1972); and V.S. Naipul, *A Bend in the River* (New York: Alfred A. Knopf, 1979).
30. For more on these sufferings, see Peter Marris, *Loss and Change* (New York: Pantheon, 1974).
31. See Denis Goulet, "The High Price of Social Change—on Peter Berger's Pyramids of Sacrifice," *Christianity and Crisis* 35: 16 (13 October 1975), pp. 231-37.

and human damage inflicted by the factories of Prai: young people became ashamed of their culture, workers wasted their money on trivial goods—Western-style permanents, perfumes, and blue jeans—and everyone lived competitively in atomized, destructive fashion. In a word, community was gone. With the help of advisors from a nearby university, they worked out a solution consisting of a novel form of aquaculture. This entailed cultivating edible cockles, thanks to the adoption of suitable modern technologies and innovative systems of cooperative labor. The achievement of Kuala Juru's villagers is remarkable: for in order to defend their traditional values they created a new way of being modern, an alternative to the standard pattern their government sought to impose upon them.[32]

Thus far I have examined four realms in which mainstream development models are bankrupt: equity, employment, dependence, and human costs. The more important question, however, is why these models have failed. After raising such high hopes in their promise, why have industrial growth models delivered such paltry results in their performance?

5. Reasons for Failure. The old strategies failed for two reasons.

(a) First, they were exported from the United States and Europe to societies culturally, psychologically, socially, and politically uncongenial to them. Most agents of change were insensitive to these differences. Introducing the wage system and the commercial mentality, for example, to people who have lived for centuries on the edge of subsistence,[33] shatters their fragile social cohesion. It breaks down constraints which protect vulnerable communities from the depredation of selfish and ambitious individuals. One development economist mindful of this delicate balance is Albert Hirschman who, as long ago as 1958, urged developers not to impose ego-focused images of change on societies favoring group-focused images of change. "Considerable care must be taken," he wrote,

> not to violate the "image" of change that alone is acceptable. This belief or suspicion, however mistaken, that a project will lead to individual enrichment rather than to collective benefits may easily spell its failure . . . .[34]

---

32. See Lim Teck Ghee, "Fishermen Find a Way," *International Development Review* 20: 2 (1978/2), pp. 45-7.
33. On this, see Robert E. Gamer, *The Developing Nations, A Comparative Perspective* (Boston: Allyn and Bacon, 1976).
34. Albert O. Hirschman, *The Strategy of Economic Development* (New Haven: Yale University Press, 1958), p. 12.

Few change agents, however, have taken care to avoid violating the "image" of change acceptable to needy communities. Experts usually impose, not propose, their standard solutions. As a result, either their advice is resisted or their impositions succeed in a purely technical sense but damage local values beyond repair. Sound development can never come through shortcuts which violate the perceptual universe, or what I have called the "existence rationality,"[35] of culture groups. A proper mix of innovative and cooperative elements is needed if change strategies are to fall on receptive soils. Overwhelmingly, however, the circulation systems through which modernity is "transferred" from "advanced" to less advanced societies has proven dysfunctional. Nevertheless, there exists a more basic defect in development paradigms, one which transcends the faulty circulation systems through which paradigms flow across national borders.

(b) The mainstream development models exported to Africa, Asia, and Latin America are flawed in their very roots. If I may borrow an archaic expression from theologians—surely a permissible sin in the hallways of a Jesuit institution—the models are vitiated *in radice*. It is not that sound development was transplanted to places unsuited to receive it. Rather, the very conception of development propagated is distorted at its point of origin. Even for the United States, sound development does not mean maximum economic growth, uncontrolled urbanization, centralized industrialization, or high mass consumption. Psychologist Erich Fromm correctly insists that *having more* often gets in the way of *being more.*[36] The social philosopher August Hecksher, in turn, comments on pressures Americans face to buy and consume in these terms:

> It is as if the machine had made its bargain: "I will give you free time in abundance, but in return you must promise to absorb my output." The output of the machine cannot be absorbed during working hours—except in so far as one machine devours another; therefore it is the task of the consumer to make his leisure constantly busier and more active. He must go places; he must equip himself; he must invest in gadgets. The result is that leisure becomes expensive; and the more time men have, the more money they spend. They must therefore work more, and

---

35. Denis Goulet, *The Cruel Choice* (New York: Atheneum, 1971), pp. 188-212.
36. Erich Fromm, *To Have or To Be?* (New York: Harper & Row, 1976).

the life of leisure becomes a constant drive to make additional money in order to be able to enjoy more adequately one's free time. The logical result—which in fact occurs often in practice —is a household full of the paraphernalia of leisure without the time or the energy to make use of them.[37]

Many students of the United States society discern an intrinsic connection between excessive competition and consumption and the pervasive loneliness and alienation which afflict our national people. Philip Slater, Christopher Lasch, and Peter Marin all write perceptively about the problem.[38] A recent article in the *New York Times Magazine* entitled "Alone, Yearning for Companionship in America" calls loneliness a nationwide disease and epidemic.[39] Clearly, personal happiness and societal development must lie elsewhere than in the mere abundance of goods. Writing on North American Indian conceptions of life and society, Barry Lopez considers that

> Some native ideas could serve us well in this historical moment: that a concept of wealth should be founded in physical health and spiritual well-being, not material possessions; that to be 'poor' is to be without family, without a tribe—without people who care deeply for you.[40]

On economic and technical as well as on psychological grounds, the United States model of affluent growth is being challenged. Advocates of steady-state growth and a sustainable society point to imbalances inherent in a mode of development which destroys nature. Throughout the world a consensus is beginning to form that what is called "development" turns out, upon critical examination, to be a spurious *ersatz*. The Swiss anthropologist Roy Preiswerk calls it maldevelopment; the French agronomist René Dumont, misdirected

---

37. August Hecksher, *The Public Happiness* (London: Hutchinson, 1963), p. 157.
38. Philip Slater, *The Pursuit of Loneliness: American Culture at the Breaking Point,* rev. ed. (Boston: Beacon Press, 1976); Christopher Lasch, *The Culture of Narcissism: American Life in an Age of Diminishing Expectations* (New York: Norton, 1978); Peter Marin, "The New Narcissism," *Harper's Magazine* (October 1975), pp. 45-56.
39. Louise Bernikow, "Alone, Yearning for Companionship in America," *The New York Times Magazine,* August 15, 1982, Section 6, pp. 24-34.
40. Barry Lopez, ed., "The American Indian Mind," *Quest/78* 2: 5 (September/October 1978), p. 109.

development.[41] Americans who long considered themselves "developed" now suspect that they are not.[42] The global quest for alternative development strategies in the Third World strikes resonant chords within our own industrial societies. Equity, job creation, and freedom from central structures and impersonal technologies now appear as essential components of our own social agenda as well as centerpieces of Third World development programs. We have come full circle: Third World critics have rejected the bankrupt paradigms we exported to them as alien transplants. Their rejection goads us into finding new development models for ourselves.

A major obstacle blocks the quest for new development models, however, in rich and poor countries alike. We are witnessing a worldwide paralysis of creative imagination. At a time when new institutions and approaches to problem solving are urgently needed, the wellsprings of social invention seem to have run dry.

A CRISIS OF IMAGINATION

As he mused about the fading glories of the Victorian Era, the poet Matthew Arnold (1822-1888) saw his beloved England "wandering between two worlds, one dead, the other powerless to be born."[43] His dirge accurately depicts our own dilemma. Our global institutions are relics of an earlier age and no longer work; already dead, they have not yet been interred. And alternative new institutions, although often portrayed in the form of desirable scenarios, do not yet exist: worse still, they seem powerless to be born. The same practical problem solvers who concede that radically new structures are needed nonetheless expend their energies scurrying from one futile exercise in front-burner crisis management to another. "Muddling through" has now become a major accomplishment requiring extraordinary measures of lucidity, vigor, and political courage.

This state of "colloidal suspension" between a dying, but lingering, world and a still-born new universe is what I call the Matthew Arnold Syndrome. It induces an institutional paralysis which exhibits itself in several realms, now briefly examined.

---

41. Roy Preiswerk, *Mal-Développement, Suisse-Monde* (Geneva: Le Centre Europe-Tiers Monde (CETIM); René Dumont, *Le mal-développement en Amérique Latine* (Paris: Editions du Seuil, 1981).
42. Denis Goulet, "The United States: A Case of Anti-Development," *Motive* 30: 4 (January 1970), pp. 6-13.
43. Matthew Arnold, "Stanzas from the Grande Chartreuse, Stanza 15," 1855. Cited in Bartlett, *Familiar Quotations,* p. 586.

1. Disjointed Phases. Our world is prey to a serious disjunction of phases. While industrial civilization is revealing itself to be empty in rich countries, it still holds out its earlier promise to poor countries, which pursue it more avidly than ever. Oil takes Mexico to the precipice of financial bankruptcy, economic collapse, and social breakdown; yet oil continues to be hailed as the country's best economic hope for the future.[44] Unwise tourist investments thrust impoverished Caribbean Islands to the brink of developmental failure, yet island workers continue to shirk agricultural tasks and look to tourism as their savior. Many Third World leaders assert that it is now their countries' turn to experience pollution because, along with pollution, or so they think, comes industry. They brook no sermons from the rich about limits to growth for they have tasted just enough industrial growth to know that in its wake it brings power, prestige, and bargaining leverage.

2. Globalism versus Nationalism. Dissonant phasing likewise marks the drive toward a new world order. The imperatives of technology, trade, disarmament, and pollution control all presuppose some form of global problem solving or governance. Yet nationalism of the narrowest sort—chauvinistic, irrational, shortsighted, and aggressive—flourishes as never before. On the one hand, transnational corporations globalize the production of goods; on the other, their very disdain of national boundaries arouses violent nationalistic feelings wherever they operate offshore. And so it is with international organizations: notwithstanding their rhetoric about supranational loyalties, they serve as conflictual arenas for ethnocentric vituperation and the promotion of parochial interests. When hiring personnel, these organizations abide by thinly disguised "quota" systems and they conduct deliberations, not in a spirit of transcendent global interests, but in the mode of trade-offs among competing gains. To speak in more general terms, the world's circulation systems, governing flows of trade, capital, technology, and information, operate vertically, not horizontally.[45] They reward superior competition, not priority needs; and they promote the domination of strong over weak partners, not the mutuality of interests.

It is precisely in order to overcome verticality in resource flows

---

44. Alan Riding, "Taming Mexico's Passion for More," *New York Times,* Business Section, September 12, 1982, pp. 1 and 26.
45. On circulation systems, see Denis Goulet, "An International Support System for Meeting Basic Needs," *The Review of Politics* 43: 1 (January 1981), pp. 22-42.

that Third World countries demand a new economic order. Albert Tévoèdjré, an African international civil servant, urges the adoption of "contracts of solidarity" in all exchanges between partners of unequal wealth or power.[46] These contracts are designed as instruments to subject powerful actors to pressures from nonelite masses and reform-minded international public opinion. Only if thus pressured will the elite stewards of the world's circulation systems begin to accept greater parity with weaker partners in negotiating arenas. In addition to promoting parity, "contracts of solidarity" aim at assuring that resources transferred reach needy people, not the already privileged. When applied to the realm of development assistance, or to use its paternalistic designation, "foreign aid," the new normative paradigm requires what the Pakistani economist Mahbub ul Haq terms the "automaticity" of transfers.[47]

3. NIEO or BHN? The most discouraging manifestation of the Matthew Arnold Syndrome is the mutual distrust which pits champions of a New International Economic Order (NIEO) against proponents of Basic Human Needs (BHN) strategies. Their hostility is so regrettable because their respective goals of greater justice among nations and among people within nations ought to merge. A recent Third World document diagnoses the problem as follows:

> While the satisfaction of basic human needs of the people, and the eradication of mass poverty must have a high priority in economic and social development, the idea is unacceptable and erroneous that these goals can be achieved without the all-round and comprehensive economic development of the

---

46. Albert Tévoèdjré, "Contracts of Solidarity," *Labour and Society* (July 1978), pp. 256-277. Cf. also Sheldon Danziger and Robert Haveman, *An Economic Concept of Solidarity: Its application to poverty and income distribution policy in the United States*, Research Series, No. 37 (Geneva: International Institute for Labour Studies, 1978); C. Montoya-Aguilar et al., *Solidarity Contracts as Possible Instruments for the Attainment of "Better Health for All,"* Research Series, No. 39 (Geneva: IILS, 1978); I.S. Chadha and Peter Tulloch, *Foreign Commerce and Solidarity Contracts*, Research Series, No. 45 (Geneva: IILS, 1979); and Guy Ankerl, *Towards a Social Contract on a World-wide Scale: Solidarity Contracts*, Research Series, No. 47 (Geneva: IILS, 1980).
47. Mahbub ul Haq, *The Poverty Curtain: Choices for the Third World* (New York: Columbia University Press, 1976), pp. 209ff.

developing countries and the establishment of the New International Order.[48]

Mutual suspicion blocks progress toward new global resource agreements or planetary bargains.[49] Many Third World negotiators reject BHN advocacy as a smokescreen the First World invokes to avoid redistributing power and guaranteed access to world resources, central items in their NIEO demands.[50] Conversely, even those BHN advocates sympathetic to Third World demands worry that the NIEO, if carried out, will simply deliver greater resources to Third World governments without improving the lot of their people. Such conflicting perceptions stall progress in the North-South dialogue which, according to Haq, "is a long-term *process*, not an event. It will require patient work on both sides if negotiations are to succeed."[51] Haq considers that:

> The real disappointment of the first phase of these negotiations is not that the North has not accepted the specific proposals put forward by the South. The real disappointment has been that the North has not put forward any counterproposals that it considered more reasonable. The North has been content to remain frozen in an essentially defensive posture—finding fault with the agenda presented by the South, and bargaining for more time by readily agreeing to formal negotiating machinery and then frustrating all attempts to reach some meaningful conclusions.[52]

Little has changed since these words were written in 1979. At the 1981 Cancun meeting, President Reagan parried Third World

---

48. *Arusha Programme for Collective Self-Reliance and Framework for Negotiations,* UNCTAD V, May 1979, p. 28. Fifth Session, 7 May, UN Document TD/236 dated 28 February, 1979.
49. Harland Cleveland, ed., *The Planetary Bargain: Proposals for a New International Economic Order to Meet Human Needs* (Aspen, Colo.: Aspen Institute, 1975).
50. On NIEO, see Jan Tinbergen, *Reshaping the International Order: A Report to the Club of Rome* (New York: E.P. Dutton, 1976); Roger D. Hansen, *Beyond the North-South Stalemate* (New York: McGraw-Hill, 1979); and William R. Cline, ed., *Policy Alternatives for a New International Economic Order* (New York: Praeger, 1979).
51. Mahbub ul Haq, "A View from the South: The Second Phase of the North-South Dialogue," in Martin M. McLaughlin, ed., *The United States and World Development, Agenda 1979* (New York: Praeger, 1979), p. 115.
52. *Ibid.*

demands for institutional reform with soothing rhetoric about pro-
cedural studies and discourses on the magic of the marketplace.
When Mrs. Gandhi tired of Reagan's rhapsodies about the poor lifting
themselves up by their own bootstraps, she reminded him that hundreds of millions of people in India are too poor to own boots and
have no straps to pull themselves up by. Reagan never caught the
sense of urgency shown by other leaders at Cancun, leading one
American journalist to conclude: "The U.S. had been given an opportunity to demonstrate cooperation and goodwill and had failed to do
so."[53]

Neither a NIEO nor a global BHN strategy can emerge until rich
and poor nations agree that social justice is equally important among
nations and among people. The North must prove that it takes the
South's demands seriously by designing its own domestic policies in
ways which support greater equity in international exchanges.
Negotiators in both camps remain stuck between two institutional
worlds: one dead, the other powerless to be born. This impasse hints
at a darker political truth, namely, that history, even in our
"enlightened" age, remains prey to countless irrational forces.

4. Irrational Forces in History. Irrationality wears many
masks. The most familiar is violence, which shreds the fabric of national and international agreements. The Sadat and Gemayel
assassinations stand as recent examples. Actual violence is but a
symptom, however, of a deeper structural violence which renders
"rational" policy making impossible.[54] Even under relatively normal
and peaceful conditions, development is largely immune to rational
management. Unplanned results of policies turn out to be more important than those which were expected. To illustrate, Latin
American development policy in the 1950s and 1960s drew its inspiration from the prescriptions of ECLA, the United Nations'
Economic Commission for Latin America. ECLA urged Latin
American nations to practice import substitution in order to build up
their industries, save foreign exchange, create jobs, and become
technologically competitive. By and large, however, dependency has

---

53. Jeremiah Novak, "Cancun: Step Forward or Lost Opportunity?",
    Worldview, 25: 1 (January 1982), p. 10. Cf. John A. Mathieson, "North-
    South Imbalances," *The Bulletin of Atomic Scientists* (January 1982), pp.
    25-28.
54. On the differences between structural and actual violence, see Johan
    Galtung, *The True Worlds* (New York: Free Press, 1975), pp. 67-8.

simply shifted its locus. Brazil, Mexico, and other nations practicing import substitution were soon spending more to buy technology used in manufacturing goods than they had previously spent to import finished goods. Worse still, the basket of goods they produced was designed, as their earlier imports had been, to satisfy the wants of classes with strong buying power, not to meet the needs of poor masses with no purchasing power.

The most irrational force hovering in the wings of policy stages, however, is the threat of nuclear annihilation. Development loses its priority when nuclear threats abound; it loses its meaning if these threats are translated to action. During his visit to the United Nations, Pope Paul VI called development "another name for peace." He could have added that "peace" is another name for the very possibility of development.

The fear of Armageddon and the knowledge that irrational forces shape history paralyze innovative problem solving in the world. World leaders are no longer "on top of things." As stated earlier, merely to "muddle through" now becomes almost synonymous with managing problems successfully. Indeed, policy makers in the United States and Europe cast envious eyes upon Italy, as though that nation's politicians had found a formula for avoiding problems simply by not facing up to them. Shades of Matthew Arnold once again, and a new warning, if any were needed, that world development is no easy thing to achieve.

This array of global obstacles to development is matched by a no less formidable string of difficulties at work within developing countries. A brief review of these domestic barriers is now in order.

DOMESTIC ROADBLOCKS TO DEVELOPMENT

If existing international structures obstruct sound development in Third World nations, so do the actions of big powers. What the United States does to Allende's Chile, to Manley's Jamaica, and to the Sandinistas' Nicaragua does little to facilitate development in these countries. Likewise with the Soviet Union's treatment of Afghanistan and Poland. No less daunting than these external obstacles, however, are the internal barriers most developing countries face: the vested interests of ruling classes, the passivity of exploited classes, a dearth of enlightened leaders, and the intrinsic difficulty of moving successfully from local to national arenas of development activity.

1. Vested Interests. Pablo González Casanova, a Mexican sociologist, was one of the first scholars to lay bare the vested interests linking the destiny of privileged classes in poor countries to that of foreign exploiters—governments, corporations, military forces, and wealthy professionals. "Internal colonialism," he calls it, and it

> has its roots in the great independence movement of the old colonies . . . . With the disappearance of the direct domination of foreigners over natives, the notion of domination and exploitation of natives by natives emerges.[55]

Traditional privileged classes (the rural aristocracy and commodity exporters), new professionals (engineers, business executives, technicians), clerks serving the ruling classes (intellectuals, bureaucrats), and upper echelons of the military hierarchy all have high stakes in keeping their countries dependent on rich world partners. They correctly perceive Alternative Development Strategies (ADSs) as a threat to their own power, wealth, social status, and global mobility, all of which depend on their partnership with foreigners. Alternative strategies which meet the needs of the poor, make nonelites self-reliant, and respect traditional values, violate their interests and preferred norms for governing society.

Experience teaches these groups to employ the rhetoric of structural change and development for the poor while protecting their own favored position. It is such ruling groups who make development policy in most Third World countries. Therefore, the bankrupt paradigms denounced above are quite acceptable to them. Growth models are good for business executives, bankers, and real estate speculators in Marcos' Philippines, Figueiredo's Brazil, Mubarak's Egypt, and Moi's Kenya. Since these interest groups are not about to relinquish development's benefits to the masses, their domestic strategy centers on coopting demands for radical change issuing from below. One favorite instrument of cooptation, or the safe channelling of demands from below, is what the British economist Charles Elliott calls the confidence mechanism or "con mech."[56] Elliott claims that ruling groups in many countries establish mechanisms for just enough upward mobility to allow a few individuals in lower classes to gain admission to the "club" of the well-off or of high

---

55. Pablo González Casanova, "Internal Colonialism and National Development," in Irving Louis Horowitz et al., eds., *Latin American Radicalism* (New York: Vintage Books, 1969), p. 119.
56. Charles Elliott, *Patterns of Poverty in the Third World* (New York: Praeger, 1975), passim.

status holders. In order to defuse potentially radical demands, elites manipulate the propensity of socially deprived groups to identify vicariously with the few members of their own cohort who climb upward. Elliott bases his theory on empirical studies in thirteen African and Asian countries. Were we to apply the "con mech" image to the American scene, we would say that so long as one Julius Erving achieves NBA stardom or one Muhamad Ali becomes a boxing champion, the United States can safely continue to deny substantive economic and social gains to most blacks. "Con mechs," however, are benign devices in the arsenal of weapons used to suppress the poor in Third World countries. Numerous rulers resort to far less gentle means: systematic intimidation, repression, torture, and outright annihilation.

Privileged elites in developing countries suffer few qualms of conscience over national development strategies which concentrate benefits in their own hands. Themselves largely Westernized, they share the values underlying these strategies. Iran under the Shah dramatically illustrates a more general pattern: a Third World upper stratum more attuned to Western business, military, bureaucratic, and technical values than to the traditions of its own populace. It is not enough to describe the posture of this upper stratum, however; one also needs to explain the inertia of oppressed groups themselves.

2. Passivity of the Exploited. Several writers have analyzed the oppressed consciousness, whether its cause is traced to overt colonialism, economic exploitation, racial discrimination, or more disguised forms of social control.[57] One dismal conclusion is common to all such analyses: oppressed people acquire a vested interest in their own servitude. As a defense mechanism, they internalize the demeaning stereotypes thrust upon them by their master. Over time this internalized image comes to define their own identity; the stereotype becomes a crutch propping up their own fragile self-esteem. To expel the internalized self-image is a long and painful process. It is because they understood this that revolutionary leaders like

---

57. Frantz Fanon, *The Wretched of the Earth,* Constance Farrington, tr. (New York: Grove Press, 1965); Albert Memmi, *The Colonizer and the Colonized* (Boston: Beacon Press, n.d.); Paulo Freire, *Pedagogy of the Oppressed* (New York: Seabury, 1970); Ronald Segal, *The Race War* (New York: Viking Press, 1967); Rodolfo Stavenhagen, *Problemas Etnicos y Campesinos* (Mexico: Instituto Nacional Indigenista, 1979); Roy Bryce Laporte and Claudewill S. Thomas, eds., *Alienation in Contemporary Society: A Multidisciplinary Examination* (New York: Praeger, 1976).

Amilcar Cabral, Che Guevara, Mao Tse-Tung, and Nguyen Giap[58] assigned high priority to the psychological transformation of their people. A new self-image conferring a sense of worth must replace that of people who are weak, inferior, and worthless. Psychological revolution is prelude to effective action against external enemies.

Historians who study revolts, whether successful or aborted, confirm the writings of revolutionary theorists.[59] Among these studies, Barrington Moore's remarkable work *Injustice: The Social Bases of Obedience and Revolt* describes with particular force the inertia found in oppressed masses.[60] Appeals to revolt cannot succeed unless two prior conditions are met. First, large numbers of oppressed people must become convinced that changes proposed to them can succeed. This conviction is hard to come by because their historical memory reminds them that rebellions are usually repressed, betrayed, or peter out after initial successes. A second condition is that such groups must come to view their present evils as intolerable, worse than any alternative, especially one which launches them into the unknown. Exploited people who survive oppression over a long time no longer view their lot as absolutely intolerable. Simply in order to survive they have had to find ways of sublimating or, to use the evocative term coined by the Jamaican sociologist Roy Bryce-Laporte, of making "secondary adaptations" to their conditions.[61] Consequently, the leap into the dark they are invited to make by revolutionary mobilizers, or even by reforms, is almost always perceived by them as too threatening.

Great leaders must appear on the horizon to help the weak overcome their passivity and accept risk. The trouble is: such leaders are a rare commodity.

---

58. Amilcar Cabral, *L'arme de la théorie,* Vol. 1 (Paris: François Maspero, 1975) and *La pratique revolutionnaire,* Vol. 2 (Paris: François Maspero, 1975); Mao Tse-Tung, *Selected Works of Mao Tse-Tung,* 5 vols. (New York: Pergamon, 1977); General Vo Nguyen Giap, *People's War People's Army* (Washington, D.C.: U.S. Government Printing Office, 1962, publication no. 0-647570); and Che Guevara, *Che Guevara on Guerrilla Warfare,* with introduction by Harries-Clichy Peterson (New York: Praeger, 1961).

59. Eric Wolf, *Peasant Wars in the Twentieth Century* (New York: Harper & Row, 1970); John Womack, Jr., *Zapata and the Mexican Revolution* (New York: Vintage, 1968); and Ralph Della Cava, *Miracle at Joaseiro* (New York: Columbia University Press, 1970).

60. Barrington Moore, Jr., *Injustice: The Social Bases of Obedience and Revolt* (New York: Pantheon, 1979), passim.

61. Bryce-Laporte and Thomas, *Alienation in Contemporary Society.*

3. *The Death of Leadership.* Gandhis, Amilcar Cabrals, Fidel Castros, Ariyaratnes, Nehrus, and Julius Nyereres cannot be mass-produced. Worse still, great leaders of nonelite masses have an alarming propensity to get assassinated notwithstanding, or perhaps because of, their qualities. It is instructive to look more closely at these qualities.

The first is an intuitive grasp of the larger historical dimensions latent in local struggles. Gandhi possessed an uncanny ability to see national significance in seemingly modest actions—a salt march to the sea, a noncooperation campaign in a single Indian city. Nowadays internationally minded educators urge people to "think globally and act locally." This is precisely what good leaders achieve, discovering global, or at least national, meanings in lesser local actions.

A second important virtue in leaders is the ability to reconcile multiple class alliances. Guevara the doctor, Castro the lawyer, and Mao the school teacher all identified with oppressed masses and experienced their exploitation as a personal affront to their own dignity. Genuine leaders circulate among many interest groups; their appeal goes beyond a single frontier of loyalty, whether founded on class, ethnic group, region, or professional category. Nasser turned the trick in Egypt, Sukarno for many years in Indonesia, and, in their own more conservative manner, so have such long-lived African political leaders as Houphouet-Boigny and Senghor.

A third mark of development leaders is moral and physical courage. Courage enables one to run risks, to persevere in the face of defeat, to reject temptations to compromise along the way, and to face death unflinchingly. At the very least, symbolic death must be faced in the form of politically suicidal decisions necessary to preserve integrity.

Good development leaders also know how to communicate their own vision of possible success to less imaginative or less experienced masses. Brazil's Helder Camara and Sicily's Danilo Dolci overcome the passivity of peasants who previously thought their oppressors invincible. A charismatic educator like Paulo Freire instills in poor workers the credible hope that they can truly become "subjects of their own history," not mere objects buffeted by social forces beyond their control.

A final quality found in good leaders is the ability to learn quickly from their mistakes. Experimentation necessarily produces some errors, but critical reflection on the reasons for the errors can lead to a more successful next round of activities. During his Bolivian campaign, Che Guevara spent the final day of each month drawing up a balance sheet of what had gone wrong and what right in the month just expired. He called it his "Analysis of the Month."[62] Ignatius of Loyola would have termed the exercise an "examination of conscience." The point is the same: unless one learns from mistakes, one is doomed to disaster. Disaster befell Sadat: lionized internationally, he underestimated resentments in fellow Egyptians over the abolition of bread subsidies and the arrest of fundamentalist political opponents. As for Ben Bella, he gloried in his external reputation as a Third World leader but neglected the internal dynamics of Algerian politics. Thus did he alienate his old army friends, one of whom, Houari Boumediene, overthrew him.

Simply to list the qualities development leaders need reveals how rarely they are found.

My remarks should not be construed as an endorsement of Thomas Carlyle's "Great Man" view of history. On the contrary, it is precisely because sound development calls for the mobilization of mass energies that good leaders are needed. Amilcar Cabral was right:

> People do not fight for ideas or for notions inside men's heads. The people fight and accept sacrifices demanded by the struggle to obtain material advantages so as to be able to live in peace and in better conditions, in order to see their lives progress and to guarantee their children's future.[63]

Oppressed people need flesh-and-blood heroes to embody their hopes for a better life and galvanize them into action. Even dictators, from Papa Doc Duvalier to N'Krumah and Peron, have recognized the importance of personifying national aspirations around themselves. That they could so easily promote personality cults reveals how desperately Third World masses need to repose their hopes in visible leaders.

4. *The Difficult Transition: From Micro to Macro Arenas of Action.* No domestic obstacle to sound development is greater than the difficulty grass-roots groups face in "graduating" from micro to macro arenas of action. It is relatively easy to launch, even to sustain, small-scale projects which meet the needs of the poor while allowing nonelites to participate in decisions. What is far more difficult is to preserve these values when a grass-roots movement

---

62. Daniel James, ed., *The Complete Bolivian Diaries of Che Guevara and Other Captured Documents* (New York: Stein and Day, 1968).

63. Amilcar Cabral, *Palavras de Ordem Gerais* (Bissau: PAIGC Secretariado Geral, 1976), p. 34.

grows in size and takes on responsibility in wider arenas of national strategy. One can create a successful free school for peasants but fail to institute an alternative national educational system for nonelites. Similarly, it is fairly easy to operate a farm cooperative on principles of economic democracy, but enormously difficult to translate these principles into a sound national agricultural policy.

E.F. Schumacher insisted that small is beautiful. This is true enough, but development strategists cannot forget that "some big is necessary."[64] The Sarvodaya Movement in Sri Lanka is one grass-roots organization that is attempting to make the transition from micro to macro development. Thus far, this village movement has concentrated on creating its own style of alternative development action. Now that it has grown large, however, its ambition is to offer its example as a model to guide the entire nation's development strategy. I cannot here retell the story of Sarvodaya's efforts as narrated in earlier writings.[65] It suffices to recall that since 1958 Sarvodaya has spread from one village to three thousand, from a handful of members to over a million. It now faces the monumental challenge of entering the national arena and surviving with integrity. For Sarvodaya, integrity means preserving its unique values and approaches to development without being coopted by the government or making compromises with the nation's elite values. These are the very values Sarvodaya seeks to change. The movement has no wish to become a mere haven for disenchanted antimodernists, a kind of successful parallel counterculture, no matter how self-sufficient or viable. On the contrary, its goal is to serve as an alternative development paradigm for the entire nation, to lead Sri Lanka into a new way of being modern, one which safeguards national culture and traditional values. Obviously, success is far from assured.

Exceptional bottoms-up innovations like Sarvodaya face still another obstacle to success, namely, an unfavorable international climate. The late J.P. Naik, a noted Indian educator and developmental strategist, was convinced that "India could follow a Gandhian path in its national development only if the whole world, or at least

---

64. I owe the formulation, "Small is beautiful, but some big is necessary," to Johan Galtung, who communicated it to me at a workshop in Enschede, Holland, May 1981.

65. Denis Goulet, *Survival With Integrity: Sarvodaya at the Crossroads* (Colombo, Sri Lanka: Marga Institute, 1981); cf. also Detlef Kantowsky, *Sarvodaya, the Other Development* (New Delhi: Vikas Publishing House, 1980); and A.T. Ariyaratne, *Collected Works,* 2 vols. Nandasena Ratnapala, ed. (Dehiwala, Sri Lanka: Sarvodaya Research Institute, n.d.).

the neighboring Asian countries, followed the same path.''[66] Unfortunately, the stewards of power and legitimacy in the world have a large stake in resisting ADSs within Third World countries.

After this depressing inventory of obstacles to authentic development, is any agenda left to ethical strategists and policy actors? In the conclusion which follows, I should like to offer a conditional Yes as the answer to this thorny question.

CONCLUSION

Five years ago, I defined genuine ethics as

> a kind of *praxis* which generates critical reflection on the value content and meaning of one's social action. Unlike mere extrinsic treatment of means, ethical *praxis* conditions choices and priorities by assigning relative value allegiances to essential needs, basic power relationships, and criteria for determining tolerable levels of human suffering in promoting social change.[67]

I still adhere to this view. Obviously, the proliferation of systemic obstacles barring sound development leaves only narrow leverage space for the conduct of any ethical *praxis*. Ethicists find it easy to diagnose injustice and exploitation in existing patterns of world investment, technology transfer, income distribution, and land tenure. They likewise have little trouble outlining preferred futures, scenarios, or designs for society. With modest efforts they can even go one step further and start implementing a strategy for the transition to sound development. That strategy's first step consists in educating the public so as to win their intellectual and political support for a normatively better future. What comes next, however, is the arduous task of conceiving and applying new modes of problem solving.

These modes of problem solving must be qualitatively better than the old ones: they must add up cumulatively to structural transformations of global and national systems.[68] Palliatives which

---

66. Private conversation with the author, New Delhi, 1977.

67. Denis Goulet, "Beyond Moralism: Ethical Strategies in Global Development," in Thomas M. McFadden, ed., *Theology Confronts a Changing World* (West Mystic, Conn.: Twenty-Third Publications, 1977), p. 19.

68. Denis Goulet, *Is Gradualism Dead?* (New York: Council on Religion and International Affairs, Ethics in Foreign Policy Series, 1970), 34 pages.

merely treat the symptoms of the evils diagnosed are ruled out. The goal is to fashion creatively incremental solutions to problems, thereby avoiding palliatives. If it is to help in finding such solutions, ethics must work as a "means of the means." This means that development ethics must define concrete instruments which support the legitimate struggles of oppressed groups. It is futile to glorify human dignity unless one builds structures which advance human dignity and remove obstacles to it. These obstacles are underdevelopment's triple curse: mass poverty, powerlessness, and hopelessness. Ethics can be a "means of the means" and play its normative role in development strategizing by entering inside the constraints and contexts of key development decisions and actions. Ethics has a twin mission: to identify the values which ought to be promoted, and to collaborate with those societal actors who can safeguard these values while simultaneously transforming institutions and behavior in ways which keep human and cultural costs within tolerable bounds. "This is quite a large order," you will say. I agree.

If this be the proper role of development ethics, it follows that the primary source of theory and evaluation for ethicists is the experimental social action conducted by living communities of need as they struggle to assert life-enhancing values in the face of dehumanizing constraints blocking their path to human development. A few hopeful signs do brighten the horizon of a generally dismal sky. Here and there in Asia, Africa, and Latin America grass-roots communities and large organized movements confront hostile government policy and combat repressive violence. In villages and large cities throughout the Third World, exploited groups undertake collective actions which, in effect, constitute the building blocks of a new development paradigm.[69] The model is being forged in concrete struggles over specific issues, not in abstract model building conducted in antiseptic seminar rooms or think tanks. One million villagers in Sri Lanka are operating Sarvodaya's alternative educational, health, and employment systems in pursuit of such values as harmony with the cosmos, active respect for all life, and solidarity with all human beings. Peasant groups in Sonora and other Mexican states are creating their own rural banks, crop insurance programs, and other institutions to circumvent the paternalistic counterparts run by the government. In the process they have acquired a certain

---

69. For numerous detailed case studies, see various issues of the *IFDA Dossier* published bi-monthly by the International Foundation for Development Alternatives in Nyon, Switzerland.

degree of national political influence.[70] Others engage in parallel struggles: one thinks here of efforts to forge new political alliances among religio-ethnic groups in Malaysia,[71] of attempts by Brazil's basic communities to articulate their experiments with development into a program of political opposition to their government.[72]

The main lesson emerging from these efforts is that experts are not those best qualified to issue development prescriptions. The message from below states, on the contrary, that the most basic human need of poor people is the freedom to define their own needs, to organize to meet them, and to transcend them as they see fit.[73] One should not be surprised that the term "transcendence" now makes it appearance in development terminology. Development specialists now belatedly acknowledge the central role religious beliefs and normative values play in conferring upon Third World populations a sense of identity, cultural integrity, and a meaningful place in the universe. The pervasive secularizing biases of most earlier development researchers had led them to create two myths: (a) that traditional values cannot harbor latent dynamisms suited to promoting development, and (b) that a reductionist form of rationality based on science and technology is an essential ingredient of modernity.[74] These myths are pointedly refuted by David Pollock, a long-time development practitioner, who includes transcendentals in his roster of development's basic dimensions. Two years ago, Pollock convened a group of Latin American specialists to reflect on prospects for

70. Stavenhagen, *Problemas Etnicos y Campesinos;* Gustavo Esteva, *La Batalla en el México Rural* (Mexico: Siglo Veintiuno, 1980); and Denis Goulet, *Mexico, Development Strategies for the Future* (Notre Dame, Ind.: University of Notre Dame Press, February, 1983).
71. Aliran, *One God, Many Paths* (Penang: Ganesh Printing Works, Sdn. Bhd., 1980).
72. Thomas C. Bruneau, *The Church in Brazil: The Politics of Religion* (Austin: University of Texas Press, 1982).
73. I am grateful to the Colombian anthropologist Manuel Zapata Olivella for this formulation of the Basic Needs issue.
74. I have treated these subjects at length in the following articles: Denis, Goulet, "Development Experts: The One-Eyed Giants," *World Development,* 8: 7/8, pp. 481-89 (July/August 1980); "In Defense of Cultural Rights: Technology, Tradition and Conflicting Models of Rationality," *Human Rights Quarterly,* 3: 4 (1981), pp. 1-18; and "I Valori Tradizionali e il Loro Ruolo Vitale nello Sviluppo," in Roberto Gritti and Eleonora Barbieri Masini, eds., *Società e Futuro* (Rome: Città Nuova, 1981), pp. 189-204.

the 1980s. The group asked what kind of development should be sought and whether earlier policies had led to deformation, reformation, or transformation. After reviewing the history of development over three decades, Pollock concludes that any definition of genuine development must comprise four dimensions: economic growth, equity in distribution, participation, and "transcendental values." To his own question, "Does man live by GNP alone?" Pollock replies:

> Should we not take advantage of our longer-term vision and ask what kind of person Latin America may wish to evolve by the end of this century? What are the transcendental values—cultural, ethical, artistic, religious, moral—that extend beyond the current workings of the purely economic and social system? How to appeal to youth, who so often seek nourishment in dreams, as well as in bread? What, in short should be the new face of the Latin American society in the future, and what human values should lie behind that new countenance?[75]

Once again this evening, we seem to have come full circle. Our reflection began by recording the concern of thoughtful economists with ends and means. Next we analyzed structural obstacles blocking the desired end, namely, sound development. And now we are summoned to view the elements of ethics' perennial agenda—the good life and the just society—as central ingredients of sound development. Godfrey Guntatilleke, director of Sri Lanka's Marga Institute for Development Studies, wrote recently that the meaning of "development" has moved from its reductionist economic phase to ever-widening circles of inclusion, embracing first social structures, then political freedoms, and later human rights. Nevertheless, he states, we are still shying away from the overall pattern of meanings to life. We must introduce to development thinking an explicit regard for what he calls "the wholeness of experience which a society can offer." In order to do so, he adds, we must acknowledge "that the nonmaterial dimensions, the spiritual and religio-cultural component in development and change, assumes central importance."[76]

75. David H. Pollock, "A Latin American Strategy to the Year 2000: Can the Past Serve as a Guide to the Future?" in David H. Pollock and A.R.M. Ritter, eds., *Latin American Prospects for the '80's: What Kinds of Development?*, Vol. I (Ottawa: Norman Paterson School of International Affairs, Carleton University, n.d.), pp. 4-9.
76. Godfrey Gunatilleke, "The Interior Dimension," *International Development Review,* 21: 1 (1979/1), p. 3.

Development ethicists need not feel diffident or apologetic about sharing policy platforms with world bankers, international politicians, or technical experts. If timidity is not warranted, however, humility certainly is. No less than other development professionals, ethicists need to wage war against their own personal, professional, ideological, and national vested interests if they are to avoid palliative solutions to global underdevelopment. More than others, ethicists need that quality of which the late L.J. Lebret so often spoke, "intelligent love."[77] Lebret's moral indignation over injustice led him to proclaim the need for prophecy, commitment, and—yes—even love. But it had to be "intelligent love," for love without disciplined intelligence is inefficient, naive, and, in its bungling good intentions, catastrophic. And intelligence without love breeds a brutalizing technocracy which crushes people. Ethicists commit an unpardonable sin if they posit a simplistic policy choice: *either* efficiency *or* humanization. Efficiency is indispensable to those who would humanize our antideveloped world. Efficiency, however, like development strategies themselves, must be redefined so as to serve human values.

Faced with the monumental task of overcoming the obstacles to development outlined this evening, nothing short of heroism is required. Yet Henri Bergson was right:

> Heroism may be the only way to love. Now, heroism cannot be preached, it has only to show itself, and its mere presence may stir others to action.[78]

---

77. For an introduction to that work, see Denis Goulet, *A New Moral Order* (Maryknoll, N.Y.: Orbis Books, 1974), pp. 23-49.
78. Henri Bergson, *The Two Sources of Morality and Religion* (Notre Dame, Ind.: University of Notre Dame Press, 1977), p. 53.

Discussion

Q. Whose responsibility is it to identify the problems in developmental ethics that you discuss? Whose responsibility is it to identify ways of dealing with these questions? Is it the responsibility of the United States? The Western world? Or the United Nations?

A. I hope you won't find my answer simplistic, but Paul Hoffman, the technical, not political, architect of the Marshall Plan, echoed the famous remark about generals and war when he wrote twenty-five years ago that development is too important a matter to be left to development experts. And so it is everybody's business, just as disarmament is too vital and crucial a matter not to be everybody's business. Clearly, that does not mean that everybody operates in the same arena of responsibility; we all have our own arenas. And I think that if you are an agronomist working in Haiti to convert Haiti's cattle ranches into food-producing farms for starving Haitian peasants, one of your responsibilities is to know about soils, since that is your area of technical competence. Clearly, a lot of people just don't have the physical means to take on that responsibility. For example, the responsibility of the starving masses in India or Bangladesh is simply to survive, and for them, just to overcome the obstacles that stand in the way of survival is already a developmental act. So, I'm not trying to fudge on the boundaries contained in your question.

Obviously, there are specific responsibilities and generic responsibilities. Thus, if we think of the United States as a nation made up of not just governmental actors but all kinds of other significant policy actors, whether they be transnational corporations or foundations or universities, certainly all of us together have a responsibility to set up, as much as possible, fruitful horizontal relationships that will promote the goals of development. Generally, we think of our relationships in political matters as quite vertical, but people who work within institutions have an ethical responsibility to be fifth columnists. In other words, they should exercise partial and conditional loyalties to their institutions, but their higher responsibilities are to the human race. For we owe a higher loyalty to those in greatest need than to those who are well off. That's why Paulo Freire always said that if you are a well-educated person who aspires to be an agent of change, you will never work for the poor unless you work with the poor. And in order to work effectively with the poor, if you don't share their existential circumstances, you have to commit class suicide.

He is talking here in metaphoric terms, but there is no doubt that something like that has to take place.

This does not mean that educators, even in privileged situations, can't make a real contribution to development. There is, in fact, a way of being a world banker or a technical assistant or a specialist that is more rather than less developmental. The real problem is what I only touched upon: figuring out a general strategy for achieving genuinely human development obviously requires a lot of incremental problem solving. It's hard to know ahead of time whether a certain way of solving a problem is simply a palliative or a creative contribution. We live within constraints of time and circumstance. That's why I claim that ethics can be helpful in a way that social sciences or the practice of a profession cannot, by isolating the issues the way a chemist isolates a compound in a chemical solution. Professing human rights, sound development, and the priorities of basic needs means moving beyond the values of the marketplace even if you have to deal with economic constraints. For example, a hard-nosed technical expert here in Washington, Chuck Weiss at the World Bank, wrote in a professional journal that we ought not conduct technology transfer on a market basis because it will simply reinforce the gap between the richest and the poorest nations. Thus we need the creativity to come up with new systems. And if we can't get rid of the old system altogether right away, at least we should try to create sufficient space for an alternative system to be nurtured and grow in.

That's why this Sarvodaya movement is interesting. There have always been small groups that have carved out a limited area and have introduced into it a qualitatively better way of doing things. But can they grow? Can they resist efforts to crush them? Well, this group has grown and has resisted efforts to crush it for twenty-two years. But now it faces a greater danger, as its leader, Ariyaratne, described it—the danger of being embraced by the government and by friendly supporters. His question is, "Can we survive with integrity and remain a grass-roots, nonelite operation now that we have to deal with macroeconomic problems?" The problem is we don't have a precedent in developmental history in the last thirty or forty years; we don't have an organization that has been committed to the three components of a viable and just alternative form of development: (1) the priority of basic needs, other than the satisfaction of the wants of those with buying power; (2) self-reliance; and, (3) nonelite participation, even while making judicious use of experts and specialists. This is not a simplistic, know-nothing attitude that says experts have nothing to tell the masses. No, it's rather a question of establishing new and horizontal relationships within a context of vulnerability. Now, it is enormously difficult to do this even if you are only a single researcher or resource partner working with someone on his own turf. Imagine how difficult it is to achieve some measure of this in an institutional relationship. That is the general direction we must move in.

Q. You mentioned the success of the Sarvodaya movement in Sri Lanka, but in India it has not proved to be particularly successful. Do you think the application of new ideologies such as Marxism to a country like India would be beneficial?

A. The Sarvodaya movement, although it drew its early inspiration from Gandhi and its name from the Sarvodaya in India, has really become quite a different operation in Sri Lanka. It never got absorbed by the government as Sarvodaya did in India, and so it never became bureaucratized as a kind of official community development or even welfare agency.

I'm not sure what you mean by a new ideology such as Marxism. That is a very old ideology indeed, 150 years old. And even in India, Marxism has been around a long, long time, even before independence. So basically, Marxism is a Western import, just like industrial capitalism. The trouble with Marxism, as with Rostow's stages of growth, is that it has its answers before it has figured out what the problem is. The problem is the powerlessness and vulnerability of the masses, not a right conception of the so-called laws of history. So the experience of the Naxalites in Bengal and Orissa is very tragic. The lessons learned by Mohanty, who studied this area, indicated that most Marxist mobilizers tend to be very elitist, tend to be very vertical. And they blame the masses for having false consciousness, for not understanding laws of history. *They* don't understand the consciousness level of the masses, and so they'll organize armed rebellions, and when the repression comes, they either run off or they get slapped in jail. And who gets stepped upon the next time around? It's the masses, it's not the organizers. Thus there is something just as alien in Marxism as there is in other Western political conceptions, except, of course, to Westerners.

That doesn't mean that Marxism does not have important mobilization strengths, namely, that it points to class division, and it provides a sharp analysis that attempts to explain economic exploitation directly and not merely indirectly. But I don't view it as significantly more relevant than any of the others. India has now undergone the experience of having played around with Marxism and all kinds of other "isms"; but the model that's going to work for any country is one that it creates itself. It will inevitably be a hybrid model, a syncretistic model. And I'm sure that any eventual model will contain elements of Marxism in its growth strategy. Going back to Pollock's notion that despite the differences for each country and perhaps for each region, four essential elements of development remain: economic improvement or wealth creation, participation, equity, and transcendentals, you find that there is enormous room for relativization here, for different mixes creating different models.

Q. You spoke about maldevelopment of the industrialized world, the United States, for example. But when you spoke of hope developing in communities where the members took an ethical stance in the practice of development, you cited primarily Third World examples. Do you have any examples in the industrialized world, where we suffer the same maldevelopment, of similar breakthroughs that you might point to?

A. I don't do any grass-roots work in the United States. I do that kind of work in the Third World, and I was talking primarily in a global context. But people who do that kind of work here, groups like the Center of Concern, or the National Center for Economic Alternatives, are in a position to know what is really going on in working-class circles, for example, with the farm workers, and they see parallel breakthroughs on the American scene. But it is an enormously uphill struggle. It's a long process, and there are no magic buttons to press or wands to wave that will make all of the injustices and inequities go away. But it is rather striking to me that even farm workers in certain of the midwestern states, like Ohio, Illinois, Indiana, and Michigan, who seem to be twenty years behind Cesar Chavez's farm workers, are still willing to stick out their necks and are finding allies.

What one finds in the United States as a sign of encouragement is that you can use certain tools like public opinion, and you can find people in the professional classes, and even in the rather large middle class and significant upper middle class, you can find a lot of people who will serve as partial allies to struggling communities in need. Such people can provide access to information, to scholarship, even to services, as well as providing direct financial support.

But even the contribution of their own skills is important. I happen to be at a university, Notre Dame, where people in the Accounting Department of the Business School, partly in order to have a living laboratory, devised a program several years ago of helping indigent people fill out their tax forms. What they found out very quickly is that very poor people are intimidated by the luxurious surroundings of a university campus. The academic types figured out quickly that people are not going to come to us, we've got to go to their neighborhoods. Once they started filling out their tax forms, the university people began to discover lots of other complications. In other words, if we want to gain entry and access to the poor, we have to show that we are not out there to judge them or hassle them. These people have lots of experience with social workers and welfare agencies prying into their privacy. We have to learn how to relate to people who fear bureaucracies, and with very good reasons for fearing them. We have to learn, in effect, without using the word, how to approach others as vulnerable people ourselves. Thus, this particular project turned out to be a useful service not only for the recipients, but also for the university people, by providing a necessary pedagogy in acquiring a developmental mentality. That's the kind of parallel I see within the United States.

José Zalaquett

Human Rights and the Moral Dimensions of International Conduct

José Zalaquett is an author, and former chairman of the Executive Committee of Amnesty International. He gave this lecture on November 2, 1982.

VALUES AND INTERESTS

Ladies and gentlemen, while reflecting on the general topic of this series of lectures, the moral dimensions of international conduct, I found myself trying to remember a sentence that would synthesize the complex question of values and motivations in public life. In fact, I came up with two such sentences, which I can trace back two years and twenty-five years, respectively. Clearly, they had made a great impression on me, for they were so readily on call. One is by former Secretary of State Cyrus Vance, the other by Saint Augustine. Mr. Vance said in a commencement address at Harvard in 1980, referring to America's foreign policy, "In the long run our interests and our ideals coincide." We are reminded (I believe by Lord Keynes) not sadly, but realistically, that in the long run we shall all be dead. But the long run is made up of very small units of day-to-day, consistent short runs, which brings us to Saint Augustine, or rather to my high school religion teacher, who quoted him back in 1957. I take his word for the accuracy of the quotation. Saint Augustine said (I remember the quote in Spanish and translate it): "If you don't live according to your convictions you will end by changing your convictions accordingly."

Both statements, it may seem to some, involve a truism of sorts. For what are values (and I take ideals, in the context of Mr. Vance's quote, to mean the attainment of goals consistent with your own values), what are values if not the expression of what a community considers to be the guiding principles that better protect in the long run the basic interests of that community and its members? Or put the other way around, isn't it our interests that shape our values, isn't it the perception and practice of basic interests, when carried out on a societal and historical scale, that becomes the stuff out of which values are formed? The question of the origins of values is certainly very intriguing, but what I find so telling in those two remarks is not their scientific validity but their patent wisdom and their policy and political implications. In effect, by saying that in the long run our interests and our ideals coincide, Mr. Vance was addressing the key issue in a continuing debate about foreign policy: that is, what relative weight to give to moral considerations and national interest considerations? He was implicitly stating, first, that in the long run there is no incompatibility between values and national interest. Second, by saying that, he was reassuring those overly concerned for the protection of their own or the perceived national interest by suggesting that these would be better served if one is guided by one's own values. Third, the reference to the long run implies room for tactical flexibility, but flexibility—and here we are once more back to Saint Augustine's sentence—should be a function of the overall respect of values and not be such that in the end you deviate from those values and end up by changing them.

Values and interests may coincide, but the question for us tonight is, are there international values by which to guide our conduct, and whose interests would such values represent? I would argue that in our present world a set of basic values of universal acceptance, representing the interests of ordinary men and women, is slowly but steadily being forged. Internationally recognized human rights are the main component of such a set of values, and governments and individuals alike, although with different degrees of responsibility and in different ways, are being called upon to observe and implement the values embodied in the human rights system.

THE EVOLUTION OF HUMAN RIGHTS

Let us begin by attempting to summarize the evolution of the human rights idea and to characterize the human rights issue and the human rights movement as they are known today. Progress in the history of human rights is usually marked by certain milestones: declarations, covenants, bills of rights. These are well-crafted, high-principled documents that seem at first reading to be the products of untrammelled light and the diligence of learned scholars. Yet, the driving force behind these documents has invariably been the struggle of peoples everywhere demanding recognition and respect for their rights. It may thus seem arbitrary to restrict the historical overview of human rights to any particular region or period of history. For the purposes of argument, however, our specific interest is to understand better the more direct historical antecedents of the human rights movement and legislation as they exist today.

From this point of view, it makes sense to confine the following historical considerations to the Western Judeo-Christian world in modern and contemporary times. It is in this context that the most distinctive feature of the whole human rights perspective evolved, that is, the placing of limits and duties upon the authorities and the community, nationally and internationally, based on the paramountcy of certain rights of the human person. Back in the twelfth and thirteenth centuries, men demanded and won limits on the authority of the king or prince. Later, rights were demanded from the colonial power or, after independence or reform, from the new constitutional nation states in Europe and the Americas. Laborious daily struggles and the insights of political philosophers inspired one another throughout this process. As a result, by the mid-nineteenth century, what has been recently termed the first generation of human rights was well established in the legislation of various countries.

Not everyone was entitled to this first generation of rights, which were civil and political. They were, to a large extent, rights for certain men. Their persons, the privacy of their property and affairs, and their freedom to participate in the associative life of the community were deemed worthy of respect and protection by the state apparatus they themselves controlled. But women did not enjoy the same rights nor were these rights considered applicable to all races or all social classes. Since those days, our common history has been, to a significant degree, the history of battles to end discrimination and to extend these basic civil and political rights to everyone. The central actors of these battles have been those who have asserted their own rights: workers and peasants, women, religious believers, nations, ethnic groups, indigenous populations, and various so-called minorities which more often than not are actually majorities. Together with the increasing formal recognition (and I say *formal* recognition because they were consecrated in law but not necessarily observed in practice) of civil and political rights for all, a so-called second generation of rights began to be formulated in the second half of the nineteenth century. These included economic, social, and cultural rights, e.g., the right to employment and to fair working conditions, the right to a standard of living that ensures health and well-being, the right to social security, the right to education, to participate in the culture of the community, the special rights of motherhood and childhood.

But it was not until after the Second World War that both the first and second generation of rights were internationally recognized. Shaken by the barbarity of that war, the independent nations at that time moved determinedly to prevent those horrors from ever happening again. Soon after the establishment of the United Nations, work on the drafting of the Universal Declaration of Human Rights began. Proclaimed by the United Nations General Assembly in December, 1948, the Declaration leads off with the following statement: "Whereas recognition of the inherent dignity and of equal and inalienable rights of all members of the human family is the foundation of freedom, justice and peace in the world..." These words link world peace and respect for human rights. The implication is that world peace and stability do not rest only on the security of governments or arrangements among governments; it is the freedom and security of citizens of all countries that is the foundation of world peace. The cruel experience of the Second World War dictated such conclusions, thus providing the basis for establishing the human rights question as a matter of legitimate international concern.

The existing political and economic structures, however, both national and international, did not allow the world to live up to its postwar vision. The real actors in the world arena at that time were the countries of the North. Africa was still largely under colonial rule; the Latin American countries remained on the periphery of the world scene, reflecting the marginalization suffered by the majority of their own people. During the Cold War years, there was hardly room on the world agenda for the furthering of international human rights. The arms race, all-out ideological confrontation, and circumscribed proxy wars marked the relationship between the two poles of world economic, political, and military power. While the fact that the world is one single stage, one single arena, had been dramatically underscored by two world wars, and while this very fact constitutes the basic assumption on which the United Nations was established, it was the 1960s that clearly impressed that reality in everyone's mind. Throughout that decade, the world witnessed the increasing clamor of the oppressed majorities. The tumultuous process of decolonialization unfolded on the African continent, paralleled by popular revolts seeking major political and economic changes in many countries of Latin America. Similar processes occurred elsewhere in the Third World. The development of this revolution of expectation among the most backward sectors of less developed countries took place in the 1960s in a special international context, made up of the North-South tensions and dialogue, implicit recognition of military parity between the super powers with their incipient efforts to limit the arms race, and the emergence or consolidation of various poles of economic, political, and even military influence on an international scene where there had previously been but two.

Other important factors included: the proliferation of internal political conflicts in numerous Third World countries and the consequent rise of strong dictatorial regimes in many of them; growing alarm over the danger of environmental pollution; increased political awareness within various creeds (particularly Christian ones), a reformulation of the role that the churches ought to play in the denunciation and elimination of the structural causes of economic and social injustice. This list of issues seems familiar now, but in the 1960s these concerns were just storming onto the international stage. As a reaction to these developments, in the early sixties, voices were increasingly heard throughout the world invoking human rights to denounce situations of intervention or repression and to demand liberty, equality, and justice. The allusion to human rights began thus to be employed as a reference to a tentative body of universal moral standards, not always defined or understood in the same manner, in order to reinforce the legitimacy of the protesters' demands. International attention during this period was stimulated by a number of events which acted as a catalyst and increased international awareness. Both the invasion of the Dominican Republic by United States marines in 1965 and the invasion of Czechoslovakia by Soviet Union troops in 1968 mobilized large sectors of world opinion around questions of relations among states and of self-determination of peoples. In the second half of the 1960s, the emergence or evolution of regimes such as those in Indonesia, Brazil, and Greece, and the continuing racist character of the government of South Africa, caused numerous voices to be raised in defense of human rights.

An important benchmark in this country was, of course, U.S. intervention in the Indochinese conflict, and the profound questioning it provoked among U.S. citizens themselves with respect to their own values and their government's foreign policies. In the early 1970s, the proliferation of repressive regimes in various countries in the Third World, particularly in South America, and the development of dissident movements in Eastern Europe and the Soviet Union, marked new steps in the rise of international interest in the topic of human rights. Finally, the declared intention of the Carter administration to make human rights a priority of U.S. foreign policy (whatever the judgment may be about the actual human rights record of that administration) further contributed to international interest in the topic and added to the controversy around human rights questions.

It is in this whole setting that, in the early to mid-1960s, the human rights issue as it is now known began to develop around the activities of ordinary men and women. Many new international actors had appeared while international and economic and political power centers spread. The world became one single arena, one single complex web of interdependence or "interconnections." As people everywhere realized this fact and the extent to which domestic conditions, including respect for human rights, depend on external factors, they started taking more interest in international affairs and from there, many moved to international activism. Thus, growing interdependence and the communication revolution have raised the world's awareness of the fact that we are one single human community—a tentative, conflicting, and seemingly nonviable community, but in the end, a community.

Any community that becomes aware of its existence starts formulating basic values by which to guide itself. Seen in this light, the Universal Declaration of Human Rights and other international human rights documents constitute the first attempt on the part of the community of nations to build up a system of values of universal acceptance. Those international instruments or documents are therefore the starting-point for the international human rights movement, the point of reference. But it was not, as I said, until nongovernmental groups, men and women in the streets, became involved in human rights action as opposed to norms, that the language of human rights and the reference to the Universal Declaration became household notions. That is how the international movement for human rights in the past fifteen to twenty years shifted its center away from organizations such as the United Nations to ordinary individuals who, it has been proven, were better prepared to place their system of values on the world agenda. Also in these last two decades other central items, closely linked to the human rights question, appeared on that international agenda: peace and disarmament, protection of the environment and of national resources, the search for a just economic order, and freedom from extreme want. These issues, too, may be seen as expressions of concern by a nascent global community that seeks to protect the common nest from being fouled or blown up, and that endeavors to use its resources for the benefit of all. Centered on these basic concerns—human rights, peace and disarmament, protection of the environment—international movements involving hundreds of thousands of ordinary men and women have been organized, new areas of study have been developed, intergovernmental and governmental activity has proliferated.

TOWARD UNIVERSAL NORMS FOR HUMAN RIGHTS

Let us turn, after sketching the evolution of the human rights question, to my contention that a system of basic values which is universally accepted is gradually being forged and that it takes the form of international human rights norms. To what extent can one affirm that human rights are universal, knowing as we do the vast differences—political, ideological, social, economic—that are to be found among the nation states of today? How can it be said that freedom of expression means the same in the Netherlands as in Czechoslovakia, that political rights are conceived of similarly in Saudi Arabia as in Canada? To these questions we may respond that the international human rights documents which contain these norms were agreed upon after a long drafting process involving complicated political bargaining. As a result, there are built-in ambiguities and generalities in the drafting of the respective provisions wherever consensus could not be reached. Summarizing the normative quality of the Universal Declaration of Human Rights, we find different norms expressed more or less strongly according to the greater or lesser degree of consensus achieved. So when we talk about the "universal" value of human rights, we use that term advisedly but with a realistic eye on the various degrees of consensus that have shaped the provisions of the Universal Declaration.

Let me be more precise. The consensus which is now expressed in the Universal Declaration and in the United Nations covenants, and other major regional and international human rights instruments, consists of five general points. In the first area there is an absolute condemnation of the most extreme forms of privation of freedom and degradation of the person, namely, slavery and servitude; on this, you find East and West in agreement. There is also an absolute condemnation of extreme forms of intolerance: the denial of freedom of thought or religion, at least insofar as holding views goes (expressing them is another matter entirely, involving many nuances). Within this first area, we find in addition agreement on the absolute condemnation of extreme forms of defenselessness of the individual before the state, namely, torture and the denial of due process, at least at a minimal level. Torture is condemned even more strongly than killing, not because anyone would not prefer to be tortured rather than killed, but because there is this element of extreme defenselessness: the person being tortured has first been rendered completely defenseless. This universal condemnation of torture in theory doesn't mean, however, that the practice of torture has been abolished, but only that the values defended by the condemnation are deemed to be of universal validity.

The second area of consensus expressed in the Universal Declaration and other instruments is the protection of life, personal freedom, and citizenship, apart from (and here's the rub) lawful exceptions. Life, citizenship, and personal freedom are protected everywhere and deemed worthy values. The lawful exceptions are the problem. What is considered a crime in some countries represents perfectly innocent behavior in others. And what is punished with very severe penalties in one country may be only a misdemeanor elsewhere: these differences point to different values. Actually, the way human rights norms are constructed allows for these differences though, of course, they are not meant to become loopholes for abuses against the absolute values referred to before. You cannot, for instance, permit the condemnation or killing of a person because of beliefs that person holds, nor can you permit killing through torture. In other words, the first set of values remains absolute. But certain countries interpret these norms as allowing them to apply the death penalty for an economic crime, for instance, which would be punished less severely (perhaps by a fine) in other countries.

Let us move now to the third area of consensus. The second one, as we have seen, is already less absolute, and allows of lawful exceptions. The third one involves the general affirmation of certain freedoms and inviolabilities: for example, freedom of expression, of movement, of association, the inviolability of the home and correspondence, and the privacy of personal affairs. The real content of those values, however, what is to be understood by freedom of expression, is not defined. Does it mean the private and plural ownership of the mass media, or having the party express the will of the people through the official organs? Interpretations vary. In addition, these rights can be restricted by an appeal to higher values like national security, morality, or public order. There is, in fact, no precise agreement as to what constitutes these values in different societies. Indeed, martial law, state of siege, or the invocation of national security are the grounds in many countries for the derogation of rights that are accepted as valid in principle: they seek refuge in the alleged exception, arguing that they have a case for actually applying the exception rather than the rule.

The fourth area of consensus is a very general endorsement of the democratic model, political participation, i.e. that governments should be elected by the people; but the respective norms are not precise enough and the vagueness allows many different regimes to contend that their particular governments are indeed an expression of the will of the people, or at least represent a transition toward that after a period of social turmoil.

A fifth and final area of consensus is the assertion of social, economic, and cultural rights. These rights have perhaps the weakest support in the international human rights documents. They are put forward as goals to be attained progressively through internal effort and international cooperation. Thus, different governments with varying economic policies can argue that they are aiming precisely at those objectives but that more time is needed, maybe ten years, maybe twenty.

These internationally recognized human rights correspond to the various levels of consensus we have just summarized. Such consensus may seem rather slender and unimpressive; yet it is arguably the largest explicit ideological consensus ever reached by humankind. Thus we may affirm that the human rights normative system—that is, the norms contained in the major international human rights documents—does enjoy a degree of universal acceptance (which does not mean, of course, universal observance). We know well that acceptance of a norm can be mere lip service and can coexist in practice with flagrant violations of the same norm.

Ideological differences, as I said, are to a large extent built into the norms themselves, in that they account for the vagueness of the norms or for exceptions to them. Still, this consensus is dynamic and grows through the activism and scholarly work undertaken within the framework of human rights advocacy. Let me give an example. The persistent activity of the human rights movement has established the principle that you cannot punish a person according to an internal law, no matter how formally legitimate that law may be, if that person is engaged in the exercise of an internationally recognized human right. That limits the scope of, say, what in an Eastern country might be considered hooliganism or an action against the state. Certain regimes are still not prepared to accept the idea that peaceful dissent is legitimate, and they may incarcerate those who engage in it. But they are being increasingly pressured by the human rights movement in the international community to observe the norm which says that people should not be put in prison for exercising their human rights. The movement is saying, in effect, that such "lawful exceptions" cannot be merely pretexts for denying the exercise of one's rights. Another example would be the meaning of democratic elections. We have a long way to go before there is universal agreement on basic principles for free elections, but it is getting more difficult for regimes to call their state elections legitimate when they do not meet the standards gradually set up by the international community as valid criteria for the fairness of an election.

This is the kind of thing I mean when I say that the consensus on human rights is dynamic. Indeed, the universality of human rights, in theory, and (especially) in practice, is one of the key questions that has to be considered when we address the general topic of these lectures—the moral dimensions of international conduct. Is there in fact an international law system? Are there international values? I would claim there is a gradually but steadily evolving system of universally accepted values. Their universality is further reinforced by several factors apart from the existence of covenants and documents signed by most governments. First of all, major creeds and religions accept explicitly or implicitly the compatibility between human rights norms and their own moral visions.

Let us take, for example, some pertinent elements in the Christian tradition to illustrate this point. Though it is highly questionable, of course, whether one can speak of a single Christian tradition without making important distinctions among the various sects and churches that embody that tradition, still it is important to point out certain aspects of the Christian vision, if we may use that phrase, which can help explain the position on human rights adopted by both the Catholic Church and certain Protestant churches and international ecumenical groups during the last two decades. Here are a few of those commonly agreed upon positions: (a) Human beings possess a transcendental worth not subordinate to any other end. Persons cannot be made instrumental to social and political arrangements. Human beings precede the state. (b) Human dignity is inherent in all individuals. Rights are the conditions for the realization of human dignity in action. (c) Religious freedom stands preeminent among human rights. (d) A preferential option for the poor should take precedence over economic liberty purchased at the cost of extreme want. (e) The social function of the church is to endorse and to encourage rather than to enact and to enforce. Consequently, there is less concern in the church's approach to rights with legal than with moral issues of enforcement. (f) In an effort to consider all the dimensions of human dignity, civil and political rights as well as economic, social, and cultural rights are equally stressed. (g) This is done in a way that seems to respond to a harmonious vision of social life but perhaps without sufficient reference to the reality of conflict. This is probably the result of the Christian conviction that love can be a source of reconciliation and conflict resolution. (h) Finally, churches stress that the transcendental nature of the human person is incompatible with purely materialistic systems or lifestyles.

These are some of the elements that can be considered common to the Christian vision, if you'll permit me that inexact expression; most of these have been consolidated, in fact, within the last couple of decades. While these notions are not exactly equivalents for the principles of human rights, they are perfectly compatible with them. Furthermore, explicit statements by church leaders have used human rights language and have stressed the compatibility between church teaching and human rights. Human rights may thus be developing into a kind of universal lay ethics compatible with other ethical systems. International human rights activists find in these norms a solid common moral reference, albeit a narrow one, that transcends whatever other theological differences they may have.

This last point deserves further attention, for many who praise the human rights movement for its humanitarian work feel nevertheless that its viewpoint is rather narrow-minded and naive. Torture, political imprisonment, or starvation, it is said, are just symptoms of deeper problems whose root causes the human rights movement neither analyzes nor seeks to remove. In response, I would say that human rights activism is, of course, but one of numerous possible approaches to questions of justice, progress, or constructive coexistence. Many avenues have been taken in addressing such questions, including trade union membership, party politics, public interest groups, and educational efforts. All these approaches are both legitimate and important, but there is no reason for various types of involvement to be mutually exclusive. Most human rights activists have, in fact, specific political persuasions, and are active in arenas other than the human rights movement. So far, the movement has not turned into an all-encompassing sect or set of dogmas, and it is essential that it not. Seen in this light, the human rights movement can be best considered as an implicit alliance for a specific set of actions, an alliance among people of many persuasions who may indeed hold opposing views on other political matters. The tacit understanding among them is that conflict will continue to mark the course of human events, but that certain essential values can and must be affirmed as essential to life and society. To achieve that goal, it is important to act on the basis of consensus, even a relatively narrow one like human rights. This universality or common ground beyond political differences that exists among human rights activists is another argument for the validity of human rights themselves.

A third element that contributes to the universality of human rights, in addition to the religious and ethical bases, is the contribution made by the mass media. By increasing their coverage of human rights issues, and by accepting as credible the information coming from the main human rights organizations, the mass media have contributed to making human rights a familiar notion and a daily concern.

There are, of course, other international values apart from those contained in international agreements on human rights. I argue that human rights represent the main component of this growing common pool of international values, but there have been other contributors to it as well. We find these other values implicit in certain key issues that have found a central place on the international agenda of vital concerns, concerns relating to subsistence, the security and welfare of individuals, groups, and nations. I am referring here to questions of development, peace and disarmament, and the protection of the environment. These issues express central interests of the international community. In emphasizing activism on these issues, I am saying that it is truly in the interest of the international community actively to promote peace, a clean environment, and economic development. Important as these issues are, they have not yet achieved a degree of consensus in practice that would allow them to be translated into international norms. What I mean is that in the process of formation of such norms, there is a moment when certain values begin to be shared and proclaimed. But for those general aspirations and values to be made operative, there must be considerable consensus on detail. This has not yet happened for this so-called third generation of human rights. There is as yet no specific international instrument setting forth this third generation of rights. They are still being discussed in theory. If the first generation covered civil and political rights, and the second, social, economic and cultural rights, the third generation would go beyond these to include the right to peace, the right to development, and the right to a clean environment, among others. But how do you translate such "rights" into functional norms for the international community at this time? As we have seen, even social and economic rights (the so-called second generation) have proved difficult to put into operation (to be enforceable or justiciable, to use more technical legal terms). Still, this third generation of rights is slowly taking shape, and may eventually crystallize into feasible norms.

WHOSE RESPONSIBILITY ARE HUMAN RIGHTS?

Having established now the fact that there are universal, international norms for human rights, I would like to turn to a second question. What role do these international values play in the actions of governments and individuals? In other words, whose behavior are international norms supposed to regulate? First and foremost, these norms are aimed at regulating the behavior of signatory states, and, more precisely, of the governments of those states. For historical legal reasons, human rights aimed primarily at protecting the individual before the state and not the individual before another individual; for the latter, each nation has its own legal system. Now it is true that individuals can and often do attack the values which human rights norms are supposed to protect, for example, the case of contemporary forms of terrorism. But it is precisely the function of the state apparatus (the judiciary, the police) to defend citizens against these attacks, which are outlawed by national legislatures and punished by national courts. The same crime, whether committed by governments or nongovernmental groups, should receive the same moral condemnation, but mobilizing the international community and international human rights machinery should be reserved for the protection of those left defenseless because the very institutions of the state that are charged with protecting their human rights are actually violating them.

That turns out to be a rather important distinction, for many people claim that the human rights movement does not condemn terrorism sufficiently. Issuing moral condemnations is easy enough, but attempting to mobilize international pressure against terrorist groups the same way one does against governments is neither effective nor very sensible, since these groups do not accept responsibility as governments do to protect their citizens against abuses. Thus, governments are agencies primarily charged with observing human rights. This implies negative and positive duties, depending on the nature of the various rights. It also implies that government not embrace conceptions of national interest which are inimical to human rights.

I would like to give some examples here of such conceptions of national security which have actually denied the very foundations of human rights. In certain South American countries, such national security doctrines evolved during the 1960s and 1970s. In studies by scholars both in this hemisphere and in Europe, these doctrines have been shown to lead to policies that affect defense but also economics, questions of political ideology and, indeed, the very structure of the state. According to these doctrines, national security is seen as the principal resonsibility of the military, and considerations of national security are given precedence over the rights of individuals. As you can see, such a conception is inimical to the whole notion of human rights, since it exactly reverses the priorities, giving consideration to the rights of individuals only after the interests of an amply defined national security are satisfied. This is, of course, an unacceptable political philosophy. Governments are not only bound to protect human rights, but they cannot legitimately develop or disseminate conceptions of national security which are intrinsically opposed to the essence of human rights. The duties of government include, furthermore, the adoption of a foreign policy that fosters human rights and does not lead to the condoning of human rights violations by other governments.

But, as we have seen, there is also an important role for the individual, and many individuals are actually taking up that role today. For at the base of the international human rights network are the numerous local organizations which have developed in the very countries where harsh violations of basic rights occur. They are working at this very moment under difficult conditions and must often suffer repression themselves. These groups vary greatly in size and in the scope of their activities, but they have much in common: they gather people from different political persuasions and creeds around the human rights agenda. They give legal, moral, and material assistance to those who have been persecuted and discriminated against and to their families. They have the best information on these questions of rights violations, and they produce reliable, documented evidence which is often the main basis for international action. They are certainly the main hope of many of their compatriots, and an inspiration for their counterparts around the world. Among international human rights organizations, some attempt to be global in their scope, as is the case with Amnesty International, which relies on the work of members gathered in some 3,000 groups worldwide; so too, the International Commission of Jurists, the International League for Human Rights, and the human rights programs of the World Council of Churches. Local and international nongovernmental human rights organizations regularly present evidence to the United Nations and to other intergovernmental bodies. Several of these bodies have greatly enlarged the scope and improved the quality of their work because of this stream of information.

The last question I would like to address is whether the establishment of norms for human rights involves a correlative duty for individuals. This is a question filled with political and ideological implications, for many governments have stressed the duties of citizens as a way of putting aside the question of human rights. Still, it cannot be denied or ignored that there is a correlative duty for every right. Individuals have the duty to respect the rights of others, and the duty to promote human rights. Such duties, however, are more moral than legal, in the sense that they are not enforceable unless an individual so blatantly disregards the human rights of others as to be guilty of criminal conduct. This question needs to be studied further, for the issue has up to now been so intertwined with political and propaganda issues that it is difficult to extricate it.

Now let me summarize. There were two basic assertions that I wanted to substantiate tonight. First of all, that there is in fact an international system of values, that such an international system of human values is of universal validity. Second, the promotion of human rights is a task both for governments and for ordinary men and women. These statements seem simple enough, and would hardly appear to need a fifty-minute long substantiation. Yet they constitute the very ground for the formulation of all other moral considerations concerning international human rights. There are, of course, many other items that are of great interest and need to be discussed, and I hope you will raise some of them during the question period: for example, the moral foundations for foreign policies based on human rights, or the agenda for future human rights action and research.

Discussion

Q. How do you answer the following argument? This is not my argument but it is an argument voiced by some, namely, that the right to be free from torture and the right to free speech are clear enough, and there should be no question about them. But some of the rights in the Universal Declaration, such as the right to have a job, and the right to a paid vacation, even the right to eat, are unrealistic. For example, if the government of Bangladesh—and I'm not saying it does this—but say the government of Bangladesh were to arrest people illegally, torture and kill them, then that government should be criticized. But, can one criticize the government of Bangladesh for not being able to provide jobs and food and vacations for millions of very poor people there?

A. Well, precisely as I said, certain rights have relatively less normative strength in the international human rights documents, because the consensus about them was not sufficient to formulate them in a manner that is enforceable or operative. Those endowed with lesser strength are the social and economic rights, except for labor rights, where the International Labor Organization has developed a set of standards that is very rich and complex— over 150 conventions and recommendations. Those standards in the ILO system, however, are largely designed for those who are already employed, and they regulate the relationship between the employer and the employee. They do not address the more critical question of how to have access to employment, that is, the question of whether there is a right to a job, which is different from having rights as a worker. That question is not really addressed by the ILO conventions in any substantive way, because it cannot be formulated in an institution made up of workers, employers, and governments of all parts of the world with very different political systems. But to your question, let me say that it is indeed more difficult to substantiate a violation of certain human rights or to provide a remedy when the rights in question are economic rights rather than the right not to be tortured. On the question of torture, you have only to prove the fact; the norms are already accepted. With regard to economic rights, you may be able to prove the fact of starvation, but you have yet to prove the connection between that fact and the actions of individuals who bear responsibility for it; there is no normative guidance for that. That does not mean the elimination of starvation should be placed somewhere below the elimination of torture on the hierarchy of values. As values, they should have the same moral strength. The question is how to render them legally operative so that there are yardsticks to measure compliance or violation and mechanisms to enforce these values. At the moment, that may seem impossible to achieve for social and economic rights, but for many of the same reasons, it seemed impossible in the late eighteenth century to abolish the slave trade. These things seem impossible now because there hasn't been enough bargaining and struggling with these issues as yet. I get into a lot of arguments with some of my human rights colleagues when I assert that economic rights are actually, as norms, weaker than political rights. But I'm not saying that at any moment they should be considered of less value; I'm only saying that there is a task to be accomplished yet, and you don't solve the problem simply by asserting that as legal norms they are the same; that is wishful thinking. So my point is to call attention to the task to be done, not to diminish the moral value of these rights.

Q. Are there really adequate means to enforce international law?

A. That is a very pertinent question. I will try to answer it in a general way rather than looking only at its legal implications. As means of enforcement, the state possesses a monopoly of force, and that is clear enough. You have no parallel to that in international law, aside from the fact that force is indeed employed in a de facto manner, and quite apart from the international law system. In international law you have mechanisms such as adjudication without the power to back up these rulings by force. Conciliation, fact finding, reporting mechanisms (whereby a state must report about its own compliance with human rights norms, and the respective human rights organism, say of the United Nations, criticizes or publishes the report)—all these are indirect systems of enforcement, whether judicial or nonjudicial. International bodies possess no "imperium" to enact their adjudications by force. Happily, however, the weight of these indirect methods of enforcement in international affairs grows greater every day as the world becomes more interdependent, both economically and politically, every day, and to the extent that states depend upon one another and are sensitive to public opinion.

Q. In talking about peace and placing it in the third generation of rights, you seem to be saying that it was less of a priority, and yet it seems to me that civil rights, women's rights, minority rights are useless unless we have peace, especially in the nuclear age. Do you agree with that?

A. I couldn't agree more, and actually, as I said, it is stated in the Preamble to the Declaration of Human Rights that the observance of human rights is the precondition for peace. What I was trying to say, by putting peace in the third generation of human rights, is that formulating a *right* to peace is a very complicated matter. What does the right to peace rather than the need for peace consist of? It is almost like talking about the right to happiness. How can you translate that into operative terms? Are you going to say that the right to peace consists of the right of every individual to have his or her nation demilitarized? People are not likely to agree now on the meaning of such a right. But the question is not whether the value of peace stands at the same moral level as other human rights or civil rights; of course it does. The point is that the right to peace may be called a third generation right, because unlike the first two generations of rights, it has not yet found its way into international documents. But this does not diminish in any way its validity as a moral right.

Q. You stated earlier that under the Carter administration human rights was made a priority in foreign policy. Some have argued that this caused problems, especially in relationships with the Soviet Union, where our policy drove a spike in that relationship, or in other cases, which you spoke of a little while ago, where anger at our policies may have pushed certain nations to more extreme forms of violation. Now under the Reagan administration we see a turning away from this priority, putting it, so to speak, on the back burner. Now we see in Chile and other countries that the incidence of violations of human rights is going up. Where do you see a point of balance between these two stands? Where do you think the optimum situation lies?

A. Let me repeat my contention that the Carter government brought about increased interest (and increased controversy) in the topic of human rights. Whatever the judgment you may have about the performance of that administration, there can be no question that international interest and controversy dramatically increased around this topic when the Carter administration proclaimed it their principal concern. Where the balance is to be found in this sort of policy has not yet been really studied and evaluated, and indeed, the effectiveness of the Carter human rights policy varied from one region of the world to another. I would claim, certainly, that there are good arguments to believe it was a positive and constructive policy in Latin America. On the other hand, I have found that in Southeast Asia, students of this issue find less reason to believe that the policy was successful or that it should receive good marks. But, I repeat, a serious evaluation of this whole matter is something that yet needs to be done. Personally, and without making a political pronouncement about one administration or another, I don't believe that human rights can be advanced solely through quiet means. Sometimes, certainly, you can achieve something more by quiet diplomacy. But I don't believe that human rights should be confined to behind-the-scenes activity. I believe, on the contrary, that human rights concerns should be highlighted as much as possible, unless you have good reasons to believe that you can achieve better results, in concrete instances, by using quiet means.

Q. Although I consider myself a strong advocate of human rights, I have something of an epistemological question concerned with who really determines morality. In other words, it seems rather paradoxical that at the Jesuit Community Lectures we are setting up a majority vote at the United Nations (which, of course, we all support) as the arbiter of morality or claiming that signatures on a piece of paper determine morality. It would seem to me that at least at Georgetown University there should be some other source of morality than majority votes at the United Nations. So, my question is really, how do we know what is moral and who determines morality? In other words, I think the fact that you have many signatories to a UN document or charter—they give you normative international law or even positive international law, but I think you may be overstating the case when you call these agreements universal moral norms, since what you have is something closer to honor among thieves. In short, how do we go from agreements among parliamentarians to determinations of morality?

A. There are several questions involved here. First, as I indicated, there are different levels of pronouncements from the United Nations. The moral force of a specific resolution of the General Assembly may be greater than that of a pronouncement of any other political body. But something different occurs when norms of permanent validity are set up by states which are taken to be the true representatives of their peoples. In addition, you have to take into account the three factors I mentioned which serve to reinforce the universal moral validity of the human rights movement: the principal creeds have endorsed the validity of these moral norms, international activism which cuts across ideologies supports them, and the world press has been giving increasing support to human rights concerns. I might also add that you can dispute the moral stature of any of the signatories of the Declaration of Independence of this country, but you cannot very well dispute the moral stature of the Declaration itself. Now, in the same way, the Universal Declaration of Human Rights has a moral value that goes beyond the individual morality of those who actually proclaimed it, and in addition, is reinforced by its acceptance by the community of nations, by major creeds, by ordinary people, and by the spokesmen of international public opinion. That was the only point I was trying to make.

Q. In response to criticism by several human rights activists and leftists in the United States, the Reagan administration last year advanced the distinction between totalitarian and authoritarian governments on the grounds that authoritarian regimes would be more open to democratic processes. I was wondering, in your own experience with Amnesty International, if you have experienced any major differences between those two kinds of government as far as human rights activity is concerned.

A. Speaking for myself, I must say that I just don't accept that academic or theoretical distinction. I believe it conceals a rather complex moral implication, although I don't question at all the morality of those who formulate this distinction. The troubling moral implication that I see is that such a way of thinking may tend to justify or condone the activities of certain governments (considered merely "authoritarian") which violate human rights of their citizens, on the grounds that these governments constitute a lesser evil. This gets to be a rather complicated business. When I was quoting Saint Augustine, I said that you cannot engage consistently in behavior that is against your convictions without ending up by changing your convictions accordingly. Once you start doing that, you are on a very slippery slope indeed.

J. BRYAN HEHIR

The Use of Force and the International System Today: Political and Moral Questions

J. Bryan Hehir is Director of the Office of International Justice and Peace, The United States Catholic Conference, and one of the contributors to the Bishops' Pastoral on Nuclear Arms. This lecture was given on November 18, 1982.

FORCE, MORALITY, AND NUCLEAR WEAPONS

I have been in Washington now for ten years, and I love the city; one of the reasons is that there are certain places where you can feed your mind and spirit in the midst of our world that often feeds neither, and Georgetown has always been one of those places for me. And so I appreciate the opportunity to come here and express some of the appreciation I feel for what this institution offers this city, particularly in the way of reflection on that neuralgic point where American policy and international affairs coincide, and not least of all on the importance of ethics at that meeting point.

When I was originally invited to give this lecture, I conceived of it in terms of a review of the nature of the international system, providing a series of cases that would exemplify the role of force in that system, along with an attempt to set up a moral framework for assessing the use of force. I had also intended to talk about the American Bishops' proposed Pastoral Letter, which is focused almost entirely, though not exclusively, on the nuclear question, but I had not intended to make that discussion a major part of my presentation. Over the last few weeks, however, and particularly in the last few days, it began to seem to me incongruous to come here and spend only ten percent of this lecture on the question of the Bishops' Pastoral Letter. At the same time, it seemed somewhat dishonest to have promised a broader lecture in my original title and not try to deal with certain of the wider issues.

And so with some fear of falling between two stools, let me sketch the final form this lecture has taken. I intend to talk about the international system as a setting for the use of force, or, better perhaps, as a setting in which force is used; that was part of my original intention. Secondly, I shall talk about Catholic teaching on the use of force as we find that teaching developed up to the present day. But then, thirdly, I intend to spend about a third of the lecture specifically on Catholic teaching on nuclear warfare and the relation between that and the Pastoral Letter that has been so much in the news recently. I want to set this specific question within the larger framework of the international system, but I also want to give you a chance to talk about the Letter itself, which has attracted, frankly, much more attention than we at the Bishops' Conference expected.

THE REAL WORLD:
BIPOLAR OR INTERDEPENDENT?

Let me begin then by talking about the international system today as a context for the use of force. What I mean by the international system today is the actual configuration of power in the world and the conceptual framework that is used to describe this configuration. One way to grasp the dynamics and structure of the system in the 1980s is to make a rapid comparison with the 1960s and 1970s to determine both the continuity and the differences and to see how that mix of stability and change provides a matrix for the different uses of force that can arise in the system.

For most of the 1960s, I would suggest, we lived in a classical bipolar world, a twentieth-century version of Athens and Sparta. The patterns of power were stark and simple: there were two major states with the capacity and the intention to compete around the globe. The other actors, not allied with one of the major powers in NATO or the Warsaw Pact, inhabited a kind of open territory called the Third World, which the two giants saw as a fertile field for ideological competition and/or proxy warfare. The world of the 1960s was classical not only in its patterns of power, but in its assumptions about international relations. The state was the center of power. States were ranked according to standards of political and strategic capability. But domestic politics was regarded as qualitatively different from foreign policy; indeed, one function of foreign policy was to insulate the domestic arena from outside influence. The superpower competition was total in both scope and method. The Cuban Missile Crisis epitomized the dangers of a bipolar world when the two adversary states had military capabilities far in excess of Athens and Sparta.

These clear outlines of the international system in the 1960s began to dim before the decade itself ended. The emergence of new centers of economic strength in Europe and Japan illustrated that power could be exercised in more than one way. The resistance of the Third World to being captured by either of the superpowers, and the refusal of France in the West and China in the East to let the superpowers monopolize nuclear weapons, all served to create by the end of the decade an emerging multipower world just below the level of superpower dominance. A radically new addition to the arena of power politics was the effective deployment of monopoly resource control by OPEC in the 1970s. While it was clearly a product of the 1973 Mideast War, it found its own way to exert pressure on the international system for both political and economic ends. The West no longer had economic hegemony.

New issues of resource shortages, highlighted by oil but not confined to it, and severe problems of food supply began to change the description of international politics in the 1970s. Moving beyond the classical distinction between the high politics of political and strategic issues, and the low politics of economic issues, analysts and actors alike began to speak in the 1970s of the "politics of interdependence" as an essential characteristic of the international system. This interdependence model stressed the increasing importance of political economy in world politics. These issues were exemplified and dramatized by a series of United Nations conferences in the 1970s which concentrated on the so-called international issues: trade and development, food and population, the law of the sea—rather unusual topics for international diplomacy. These transnational issues were beyond the capacity of any single state to resolve. Indeed, such transnational questions were forcing everyone to look anew at the role of the state in an interdependent world. Not only was the state faced by new problems, but it was in competition with new actors, actors I have described as "transnational actors" with their own trained corps of personnel, a single guiding philosophy, and a sophisticated communications system. The existence of these transnational actors raised increasingly important conceptual questions about their relative power vis-à-vis the state. The state clearly maintained its predominance in world politics, but it functioned now in a new context—or what was described as a new context—of international dependence. As national governments became increasingly involved in their own domestic economies, the economies themselves were caught up in the world of international economics.

The politics of interdependence now became a major theme in the literature of international relations and a topic for statesmen to contend with. For by the mid and late 1970s, discussion had moved beyond the universities. President Carter's first major foreign policy address at Notre Dame in 1977 was devoted precisely to the changes in the world produced by the politics of interdependence. The Notre Dame speech became a benchmark for foreign policy debate. Critics of the Carter foreign policy, like Professor Robert Tucker of Johns Hopkins, Professor (now Ambassador) Jeane Kirkpatrick of this university, and Senator Daniel Patrick Moynihan from within the President's own party, all argued that the interdependence of the world was at the root of United States foreign policy problems from Moscow to Iran to Afghanistan to Central America. In other words, the question whether the classical bipolar world had really been transmuted into anything essentially different was up for debate. Tucker was writing at the end of the 1970s that the real world had not conformed to the theory of an interdependent world. Rather than seeing the emergence of a new politics, we find ourselves enmeshed in the same old politics. In this familiar world, neither the rivalry of the superpowers nor the stakes have changed very much from a generation ago. Indeed, when we look at how the 1970s, the "decade of interdependence," ended, we are left with Iran, Afghanistan, and with the U.S. decision to shelve SALT II and to embark on a program of modernizing nuclear forces in Europe.

The question then becomes, what is the actual international system of the 1980s? Does it reflect the classical bipolar world of the 1960s, the interdependent world of the 1970s, or is it some mix of the two? The critics of interdependence were calling at the end of the 1970s for a return, in fact, to classical modes of thought in foreign policy, for a reassessment of the usefulness of force in world affairs, and for the reversal of attempts to make interdependence a major theme of U.S. policy and a major conceptual element in the understanding of the international system. Others, like Professor Stanley Hoffman of Harvard, pointed out that the problems inherent in reverting to the mindset of the 1960s were simply overwhelming. Hoffman argued instead that the interdependence model did describe an important new dynamic in world politics. While it would be too much to say that interdependence had transformed the nature of international relations so that the role of the state and resort to force had become outmoded, still it would be saying far too little to try to explain the world of the 1980s simply in terms of the classical bipolar model. The reality of the system today requires both categories.

If a series of events like the ones noted has illustrated the staying power of political strategic issues in world politics, the political economic issues of interdependence and the related question of the use of force in such a system are no less characteristic of the real world of international relations. A good indication of the change that has taken place, despite the persistence of the superpower rivalry, is the combination of new elements that go into the ranking of a hierarchy of nation states. There are certain states that are military powers but lack comparable economic power, for example, the Soviet Union. Other states are economic powers but possess little capacity to use force in terms of a classical conception of military power; here Japan and Saudi Arabia provide good examples. And then there are other states that possess neither economic nor military power. In this mixed system there are different kinds of force that can be brought to bear. At the superpower level, there is the overwhelming capability of both superpowers to threaten, at least, the use of both nuclear and massive nonnuclear force. One of the questions from the 1960s that has perdured through the 1970s is exactly what that capability amounts to, particularly when it is a question of nuclear force. In other words, what is the political utility of the various levels of superiority and inferiority in a nuclear relationship?

I shall come back to that question when I consider the nuclear question in more detail.

But it is also interesting to look at other potential uses of force in this mixed system, partly classical, partly interdependent. There are many instances where force has been used in the past few years within a state and has been, to some degree, insulated from the larger international system. In Zimbabwe, for example, there was a dramatic change of government, and it appears that the superpowers deliberately kept their distance. The United States allowed Britain to take the leading role in working out a diplomatic solution; neither clearly wanted to see the struggle escalated to the superpower level. Other examples of the use of force that appear to have nothing to do with the superpower struggle include the overthrow of Idi Amin in Uganda by a classical invasion from Tanzania. And even the war between Iran and Iraq, which certainly has international implications and, I suspect, probably international involvement, is being fought out on their own terrain, and whatever the involvement of the superpowers, it is more covert than overt.

On the other hand, there are certain places in the world where regional uses of force are directly tied to the larger international system. The Middle East is perhaps the best example. My point is that in talking about the use of force in the international system today, and in discussing an ethic of force, one has to distinguish between cases in which the dominance of the superpowers is clearly an issue and others which seem to be insulated from superpower competition. An analysis of the use of force in these situations would yield different results. The classical moral categories would apply in all cases, of course, but how one would apply them in light of the complexity of the larger system is precisely the point at issue.

CATHOLIC TEACHING ON THE USE OF FORCE

Having classified the various kinds of force available, I would like to move on now to talk about Catholic understanding of the use of force in an age where both nuclear and nonnuclear military power is available. I am especially interested in looking at the traditional categories of Catholic teaching on the question of force and in testing their applicability in the nuclear age. Given the setting of these lectures at a major Catholic university, I don't think it will be necessary to trace in great detail the development of Catholic teaching on these matters from the earliest moments of the Church's life to the twentieth century. I assume that the broad outlines of the moral tradition are already known. Instead, I should like to concentrate on the fact that within the last twenty years there have been two major shifts within the moral framework of Catholic teaching on the use of force, and their consequences have already been felt in the way the Church both thinks and acts in certain situations.

The first of these two shifts is the emergence of a moral pluralism regarding the starting point for evaluating the use of force according to moral theology. The dominant tradition in Catholic thought, from the time of Augustine to Pius XII, is centered on the categories of the just war as the moral justification for the use of force. From the time that Augustine developed the moral logic for the limited use of force as both politically necessary and morally justifiable in a world marked by sin, through the pontificate of Pius XII, no other moral option really existed within the Catholic community on the use of force. There was, of course, another option within the Christian tradition known as nonviolent pacifism, and there were Catholic people who held to this tradition. But they did not find legitimation for it within Catholic teaching. A just war or limited war approach developed categories of ends and means for the use of force and articulated the *ius ad bellum* and the *ius in bello* into seven distinct principles that mirrored the historical evolution of that tradition. The major shift in the past two decades has been that alongside this classical argument which would make the use of force morally justifiable and indeed perhaps morally necessary for a Christian, the nonviolent, pacifist option has emerged as a newly legitimated approach to the question of force. Thus, the moral pluralism I mentioned.

There are, indeed, two different starting points for the Christian community's thinking about the morality of the use of force. The nonviolent position argues flatly that any use of force is incompatible with the Christian vocation. The just war position argues that certain uses of force, but certainly not all uses, can be justified within the logic of Christian faith and reason. I want to emphasize that point because one of the things that will become clear in the subsequent discussion of the Pastoral Letter is that we are in for a major debate; indeed, it seems to me that it has already begun. Members of the Catholic community will differ on a number of things. We shall differ on our empirical analysis of political trends, on technological judgments about weapons systems and their effect on the political process, and more fundamentally, we shall find ourselves differing on the fundamental conception of what is morally right in the use of force. Therefore, we shall need to learn how to discuss this enormously complicated issue within a community where there are two different and legitimate starting points. This moral pluralism is reflected in the draft document of the Bishops' Letter, but surprisingly it has received little attention. The media have emphasized the hard issues of deterrence and the use of force or our judgments on the political system. But from a Catholic point of view, the affirmation of pluralism is a far more startling departure.

The second shift that has occurred within Catholic moral teaching on warfare is a move away from an exclusive concentration on the moral question of how you limit the use of force and toward a second position that can be described, for want of a better term, as the need to develop a positive theology of peace. Now, this does not represent an entirely new direction, and I would argue that it represents a bipolar conception of the teaching task. The whole thrust of the just war doctrine has been to limit the use of force in human affairs, while recognizing that the use of force is part of the human condition in a world marked by sin, in a world still organized in terms of international systems, sovereign states, which consider the use of force as an inherent right included in their very nature. In such a world, attention to limiting the use of force is obviously still a valid and necessary moral enterprise. But, if we are trying to understand new developments in Catholic thought, we must look beyond this first (and necessary) task to a second which has recently emerged: the notion that the theology of the Church, drawn from scriptural wisdom, theological insight, and moral judgment, should be developing a view of the Church as itself an instrument of peace, and of the community of the Church as peacemakers. This means developing new themes—or perhaps old themes in a new way. Thus we find a second kind of pluralism in Catholic teaching: no less concentration on the limitation of war, to be sure, but also an at least initial exploration of what one might call a positive theology of peace. There have, of course, been strong elements of such a theology in much of the papal teaching on international affairs since the time of Pius XII. Both papal encyclicals and documents of Vatican II have explored ways in which the international system might be structured in order to reduce the need for a resort to force. Behind these texts lies a conception of political and legal order that would reflect a belief that the human community is indeed one community. But all of this is not exactly what people mean when they talk today about a positive theology of peace. It is something more even than what we find, for example, in such a striking and rich document as *Pacem in Terris*.

These two important shifts: a moral pluralism that embraces both the just-war and the nonviolent approach to the use of force, and the development of a positive theology of peace alongside a concern with limiting force—these shifts have influenced not only the thinking of the Church but also its way of acting. Let me give you some examples. There are two cases in Central America where the classical conceptions of the just-war argument have been visible in the last few years. At a certain point in the Nicaraguan revolution, the bishops of Nicaragua issued a statement saying that conditions existed that justified revolution, that is to say, conditions existed which made the use of force morally legitimate. Today, with all the conflict and confusion inside Nicaragua, it is still important to realize that at a crucial point the bishops there legitimated the resort to force in a very classical way. A contrary case can be found in El Salvador. Two years ago, in January of 1981, certain parts of the Church in El Salvador (certain priests, religious, and Catholic organizations) drew up a document that was, once again, almost a classical instance of the application of the just-war theory to the right to revolution, an option that has always been a part of a just-war theology. They argued that conditions existed that legitimated the use of force. The then Apostolic Administrator of San Salvador, Archbishop Rivera y Damas, argued from the pulpit that he agreed with part of the analysis but not with all of it. On that basis, he disagreed with the contention that the time had come to legitimate the use of force. Now, I use these two cases simply to illustrate that the logic of what we have called the classical doctrine on force still plays a role in the way the Church thinks about what it ought to do in certain circumstances.

On the other hand, the emergence of a strong nonviolent movement in the Church is interesting, not least of all for the effect it has had on our own Church here in the United States. For the moment, however, I am more interested in its importance elsewhere in the international system. First of all, it is important to note that it does not mean what certain commentators have taken it to mean, namely, passivity in the face of evil. Once again, the Church in Latin America provides a good example, for its leaders like Archbishop Helder Camara have tied their call for fundamental changes in the Latin American political system to nonviolent positions. In addition to Archbishop Camara, one could also mention Cardinal Paolo Evaristo Arns of São Paolo, a less visible but no less committed advocate of nonviolent change. Another interesting case from a different part of the world is the attitude of the Church in Poland to its own difficult situation. It seems clear to me that the voice of certain churchmen, inside or outside Poland, could muster thousands of people on the streets very quickly; this kind of encouragement has been very carefully avoided. What has not been avoided, however, is the constant addressing of the human rights situation there, along with an appeal for fundamental political change insofar as that is possible. Thus in a situation very different from Latin America, the Church is once again walking a very careful line between a call for basic social change that has a revolutionary ring to it and an official endorsement of revolutionary force.

The situation of the churches in South Africa provides another and much more unpredictable example of the same problem. I'm not at all certain how the churches there will deal with this question of the need for fundamental change coupled with the question about the legitimacy of the use of force. The movement for change there is very powerful and it always holds open the possibility of the use of revolutionary force as a last resort. As the churches become more openly involved in calling for deeper and deeper changes within that society, they will clearly be faced with that moral option, and I simply do not know what position they will adopt. I do know that the Catholic Bishops in South Africa have shown enormous interest in the American Bishops' Pastoral Letter. How relevant it will be to them is another question, because the problems facing the two hierarchies are so very different. I mention these instances because I think they illustrate the shifts I have described in Catholic teaching. You have certain situations which can be interpreted very precisely in terms of just-war norms. There are other situations where the Church has joined itself to what must be described as a radical social stance that includes a nonviolent philosophy of change, and has held firmly to both elements.

THE CHURCH IN THE NUCLEAR AGE

Beyond these two thematic changes within Catholic moral teaching, there is the further question of specific Catholic teaching on the use of force in a nuclear age. Let me begin by describing the nature of the challenge that our age has posed to any teaching about the use of force. It has become a commonplace in strategic literature and in the literature of international relations to speak about the nuclear age as affecting a transvaluation of accepted norms. Twenty years ago, Henry Kissinger argued that the classical conception of force, in which every increment of physical power a state gained was expected to yield a similar increase in political influence, has become outmoded in the nuclear age. Even enormous increases in physical force no longer yield comparable political increments because the force is so great that it negates the possibility of its being a useful instrument in the ordinary ways of politics and dipomacy. There is a similar reversal of this continuum between physical force and political influence in the moral order. Even one who holds with the central tradition that certain uses of force are morally permissible must question whether this new kind of force—understood not only quantitatively in terms of megatonnage but also qualitatively in the way the nuclear barrier introduces a step into the unknown—poses a fundamentally and qualitatively new kind of moral problem for the just-war tradition. It is interesting in this regard to trace the development of the Church's attitude toward this new problem.

Pius XII was the first to grapple with it, and I think his experience parallels, in moral terms, what one finds in the political, scientific, and technical literature on nuclear power. His first instinct was to think of nuclear weapons as merely one more step in a continuum of force. The judgment then was: If you can control them, then the classical categories continue to work. He put that in hypothetical terms: If the effects of nuclear weapons can be controlled, then they can be fitted into a traditional understanding of the use of force in international affairs. What is interesting for us is not so much his judgment as the tenor of his discussion. Nothing indicates that he is dealing here with a qualitatively new problem. There is, instead, a sense of progression, applying traditional categories to a new stage of an old problem.

Pius XII died in 1958. By 1963, in Pope John XXIII's encyclical *Pacem In Terris,* an important shift has already taken place, a shift in psychology and in moral vision. Nuclear weapons are no longer treated as if they were simply part of a continuum; they are treated instead as something fundamentally different. Indeed, within the institution that has been the most consistent interpreter of the just-war tradition, you come upon that much disputed sentence of John XXIII about whether there would ever be an act of reason to consider using force in an age where force includes a nuclear arsenal. That sentence represents a major challenge to the whole moral tradition about permissible uses of force. You will find nothing in that encyclical about the state's legitimate right to defense. But you will also not find, interestingly enough, any affirmation in it of what I have called the nonviolent tradition, any assertion that the moral tradition has now become an option for Catholics. What you get instead is a shift in tenor and tone that challenges the premise that the use of force in the political arena can be contained in a way that would make it an instrument of reason.

Two years after *Pacem In Terris,* the Second Vatican Council established the frame of reference out of which we still work. The Pastoral Constitution on the Church in the Modern World first introduced what I have called moral pluralism. On the one hand, we have, for the first time in modern history at least, a clear affirmation of the nonviolent option for Catholic Christians. It is tentative, but it is there, for example, in the demand that states make provision for those who hold the position of conscientious objection. Now in Catholic moral tradition, which argues that civil law ought to reflect the moral law, you can only demand that a state make a legal provision for something like conscientious objection if you believe that this position has solid moral authority. There are as well statements in the document that speak of the need to praise those who refuse to use force. At the same time, however, there is a reaffirmation of the right of self-defense, based on the lack of central world authority. These two affirmations established the pluralistic framework in which the argument has been developed up to the present day.

It is also in this document, of course, that the nuclear question is addressed with more precision than it was by either John XXIII or Pius XII. I do not claim that the nuclear dilemma is addressed with adequate precision, but the terms are more sophisiticated. The Council speaks of "weapons of mass destruction," a term wider, presumably than "nuclear weapons," but certainly including them as the core of the definition. The document does not engage in an exhaustive analysis of whether one may ever use this kind of weapon. It reaffirms instead the traditional principle against counter-civilian and counter-city warfare, and issues a ringing condemnation of that practice, the only condemnation in all the documents of the Council. By doing so, it places Church teaching athwart the path of contemporary superpower strategy which toys with the idea that obliterating cities may be necessary.

On the question of deterrence, the Council was modest, as well it might have been. But it defined the question well. Let me paraphrase: In our age, in a way heretofore unknown, weapons are amassed for what are called defensive purposes. The logic of the argument is that weapons are only amassed for purposes of deterrence. In the careful manner in which Roman documents often use language, the Council Fathers go on to say, some claim that this amassing of weapons in fact prevents war. The Council Fathers do not say that they accept the argument, nor do they say that only fools put it forward. They merely say, some people claim this. And when you look to see what position the Council Fathers themselves take, you find them saying that, whatever the case may be with this method of deterrence, what is absolutely necessary is that the arms race be curbed. Now, I am paraphrasing rather than quoting this long text, but I think the logic of the argument has been preserved.

In those paragraphs, the Vatican Council opened up the deterrence question, and what has been going on in the media treatment of the Bishops' Pastoral Letter recently has been the continuing argument of how one tries to "close it" in any morally satisfactory fashion. Pope Paul VI added moral passion to the Church's teaching and tried to take the question of war more directly to the Christian conscience in a variety of ways: for example, on his trip to the United Nations, and by his declaration of an annual Day of Peace in the life of the Church (which we celebrate on the first day of the year). But I would suggest that he made no qualitatively new contribution to the moral argument. His categories were very much the categories set at the Vatican Council. At times he would praise the nonviolent option, giving examples of its usefulness and value. At other times he would reaffirm the legitimate right of states to self-defense. He never took up the deterrence question or argued it in any detail at all. His pontificate was enormously important for the issue of war and peace, but not in terms of developing the moral argument.

Pope John Paul II, it seems to me, has done two things. First of all, he has cast the question in his own distinctive manner, something he has done with a number of questions. It is almost as if he refuses to start where others start to discuss this question. In order to relate his position to the ongoing argument, you have to find out where he is coming from. As I read him, he always discusses the nuclear question in terms of larger categories: within the relationship of politics, technology, and ethics. This seems to be his general approach to all kinds of questions, from nuclear weapons to medical ethics. He is fascinated by the human community's capacity for technological development, and he doesn't condemn it; indeed, he often praises it, but the fundamental question remains whether technological development can be contained within political and ultimately moral categories so that its products serve us rather than consume us. Such is the context for his speeches at Hiroshima or his speeches to scientists.

Secondly, he has introduced a new degree of specificity to the discussion. This is precisely what Paul VI did not do. This specificity has two dimensions. He combines his moral and religious arguments with demonstrative acts, another general characteristic of his pontificate. Thus, if he wants to talk about nuclear war, he goes to Hiroshima so that his meaning cannot be missed. When he commissions a study on the effects of nuclear war from the Pontifical Academy of Science, he doesn't rely on the media to transmit it to our President; he sends five members of the Academy to deliver the results to him and to four other world leaders as well. Such gestures have their effect, not least of all on our own Bishops, as their own actions and statements demonstrate.

The second level of specificity can be found in the Pope's venturing directly into the argument about deterrence. For the first time since the Vatican Council, we have at least one statement from Rome. Visiting the United Nations, he deliberately entered the discussion; and even if his precise meaning is open to dispute, there can be no doubt that he wants to be part of the debate. The contribution was somewhat cryptic, arguing that deterrence, based on balance, and certainly not as an end in itself, may still be judged morally acceptable so long as it is seen as a step on the way to progressive disarmament. Reading through the whole speech, one gets the distinct impression that this statement is deliberately introduced; if you remove this paragraph, the speech flows smoothly without it. This contribution is certainly more specific than any other statement from the Holy See on the question of deterrence, and although it certainly does not close the argument, it demands to be taken into account in any discussion of the nuclear question.

To sum up, there are three distinct ethical questions that must be considered: the first has to do with the use of nuclear weapons. Are they simply more of the same, or must they be classified as something new? Secondly, the question of deterrence; here the dimensions are certainly new, but the final resolution is still uncertain. And then thirdly, there is the relationship of both of these aspects of the nuclear question to the larger question of an international order. Here the popes have gone back once again to their fundamental political argument, arguing that this new kind of danger to the world stems from a more general problem of the lack of an adequate international political system. In addition, they regularly condemn the investment of enormous human resources in military means when the human, social, and economic needs of the globe are so enormous and so increasingly obvious. This is an admittedly sketchy account of the attempt by the universal Church to grapple with the dilemmas of a nuclear age.

THE AMERICAN CHURCH
AND THE NUCLEAR STATE

In order to provide a framework for understanding the American Bishops' Pastoral Letter, let me close my presentation with a discussion of the state of the nuclear question in the United States. First of all, let me be clear in stating my own conviction and that of the Bishops that they are part of the Church, and not the whole Church. This has been clear ever since Vatican II, and the Bishops firmly believe it. So, when I focus the discussion on the Bishops, I don't mean to say that this is the Church speaking. On the other hand, given our polity, when the Bishops speak they possess a weight of authority that must be considered in the larger debate even if their statements do not bring the debate to a close.

I suppose the first question that comes to mind is, why now? Why have the Bishops decided to speak now, and why haven't they spoken before? I think there are three reasons for their deciding on this particular moment. The first reason is quite simply the impact of the papacy on them. The Bishops are quite sensitive to any continuing refrain from the universal teaching authority of the Church. It is not simply, however, a question of the accumulation of statements; it has more to do with a new sense of ecclesiology. I have seen this in the way they have debated the Pastoral Letter. There are many differences among them about the moral questions involved, but I think they have few differences on their ecclesial responsibility as pastors in this country. And so, the effect of Roman statements has been to make the Bishops aware of their pastoral responsibility to relate the Church's general concern about nuclear weapons to our actual situation in this country. It is in the light of the Council that the Bishops have developed a sense of themselves as the leaders of the local Church, and this has meant a sense of corporate responsibility for the whole country and not just for their individual dioceses. Responsible ministry within the Church has come to include dealing with as difficult and as sensitive an issue as American nuclear policy.

The second catalyst that has generated this statement, I think, has come not from above but from below. In a variety of ways, events in the Bishops' local churches have moved them to address this issue. Certain people have propelled them forward by asking what they have to say about this issue in the light of Catholic tradition, the light of the Pope's statements, and by asking whether they can afford to remain silent. Other kinds of forces are also at work, for example, the implications of their position on abortion. I don't have any doubt that for a number of Bishops the logic of their position on abortion has moved them to consider the question of nuclear warfare, but it takes time for a group as diverse as the American Bishops to see how one issue implies another and to generate ecclesial consensus on the precise connections between the issues.

Combined with these two developments, there is a third which is much less fundamental, but not insignificant. It has to do with the matter of intuition, a realization that arises from considering their own responsibility for this issue, and is an intuition generally shared, namely, that the arms race is going in the wrong direction, that things are not getting better but are perhaps getting worse. When you put these three elements together, you get a converging sense that something must be said and done. Looking back, you can almost pinpoint the stages of this developing consensus as the Bishops wrestled with these questions. The Bishops are not all at the same point, but there is pretty substantial consensus about the second draft of the Pastoral Letter, consensus at least about the direction it is taking, if not about every point in it. The first stage in this development was the entry of the U.S. Catholic Conference into the SALT II debate, when Cardinal Krol testified before a Senate committee in the name of the Bishops' Conference, laying out their position on the SALT II agreement. To a certain extent, the testimony itself was of secondary importance. Of primary importance was their need to get clear in their own minds what they wanted to say about the issue before they decided to testify. There were basically two extremes of thought that reflected some of the moral pluralism I talked about before. One group within the Bishops' Conference focused on the deterrence issue as the key moral question, arguing that though the treaty sought to limit deterrence, it basically supported a morally wrong policy of mutual terror. Thus, already at the time of the SALT II debate, there had emerged a group of Bishops who had formed a position on the deterrence argument itself. On the other side, a group of Bishops argued that though deterrence was unsatisfactory, it should not be turned into the primary moral question and that one could indeed support the treaty, even though that would mean cooperation with an unsatisfactory system. Cardinal Krol's testimony then, laid out the arguments for considering deterrence less than satisfactory but, as he put it, still tolerable. But he stressed that the judgment of toleration was not open-ended, precisely because of its unsatisfactory nature in moral terms, but was conditional on a serious effort to reverse the arms race. This testimony, though not of primary importance, set the framework for the broader discussion of nuclear arms here and to some degree in the Churches of Europe on the question of deterrence.

The second stage of development among the Bishops occurred when individual Bishops began to address this question. To date, some 85 Bishops have spoken individually on this issue, and I would stress that there is continuum here too. The Pastoral Letter in its final form will represent a consensus statement, but there is evidently a good deal of pluralism among the Bishops themselves on the question of nuclear arms. Concretely, a man like Archbishop Raymond Hunthausen is clearly in principle a pacifist who would hold for a unilateralist position on disarmament if it were necessary, though this is not his first option; moreover, he feels that the nature of the arms race is so clearly immoral that he is moved to civil disobedience. He does not attempt to pressure anyone else into taking that position, but he takes it himself.

From that position you can move across the spectrum to what might be called the "Pax Christi Bishops." These were the Bishops who challenged the decision to testify at the time of the SALT II treaty. They are as a group sympathetic to Hunthausen, but none of them has taken his specific position, for example, on civil disobedience. Thus they represent a distinct group, and their importance within the Conference is that they force the rest of the Bishops to address the issue even though the final result may not represent their position. Next to them, I would say, would be Krol himself, and his importance is not his position on the SALT II agreement, but, more importantly, his role within the American hierarchy. In a sense, he legitimates the issue for a whole body of Bishops who would probably be thought of as conservatives. His anticommunist credentials are excellent, and so he cannot easily be accused of being naive about the nature of the Soviet Union, or the situation in Eastern Europe. In addition, he has stayed with the issue. Next to him on the spectrum would be someone like Archbishop John Quinn of San Francisco. Quinn entered the debate at the end of 1981 with a major statement drawn out of the classical just-war tradition—a very different starting point, for example, from that of Hunthausen, and many of the "Pax Christi Bishops." Working within the classical Catholic tradition, he arrived at a very strong critique of the arms race itself and of the use of nuclear weapons, and a position not unlike Krol's on deterrence. Quinn represents, I would suspect, the center of the spectrum at the moment.

Next to him I would put Cardinal Terence Cooke. The public interpretation of Cooke's statement on deterrence overplayed his differences with the rest of the Bishops. His judgment on deterrence was exactly the same as Krol's, since the most he would grant was toleration. He was not quite so firm on the use of the weapons, but his statement was hardly diametrically opposed to Krol's. Moving beyond Cooke, you will find a body of Bishops who are clearly interested in this question, and worried about the ethics of means, as I would classify these questions about use and deterrence, but also worried about the ethics of ends, and who are particularly concerned about the nature of the Soviet threat. I'd say Bishop McNicholas is a good spokesman for this position. Fundamentally, he is not in disagreement with the judgment on means that is offered by people like Quinn and Krol, but he wants to stress the perplexity of making that judgment in a world in which the Soviets represent a major factor. With Archbishop Hannan, we sense another shift; he is so taken by the nature of the Soviet threat that the ethics of means is not a major part of his analysis. You might say that for him it is the *ius ad bellum* which determines his judgment rather than the *ius in bello*.

It is this spectrum, with each of the people named surrounded by a group of Bishops in agreement with them, that sets the frame of reference for looking at this document. The Letter itself is an attempt to shape a consensus from a body that is not in consensus on every point. Having Bishops speak individually to this question has been a healthy exercise of pastoral ministry, and I don't think they're going to stop taking differing positions on this question. But you can still form a consensus even within a moral pluralism that takes for granted distinctly different starting points for making moral judgments. You can forge such a consensus even when you move one step up from the starting point, with the result that you might differ on specific questions about use, for example. But you can still forge a consensus, and that is what the Pastoral Letter is basically designed to do. For there is a strong feeling that you need more than just individual statements; on an issue of this importance, there is that sense of ecclesial responsibility I have described, and there is a need to express it corporately, ecclesially.

THE PURPOSE OF THE PASTORAL LETTER

The Letter is designed to do two things. For the Bishops it is generally considered as a teaching document; that would be their own description of what they're about, exercising their teaching ministry. But they are exercising it in two different ways. First of all, they are exercising it vis-à-vis the community of the Church, where there is a shared set of premises and principles of the Gospel and Catholic theology; that is the background out of which they work. Secondly, they are exercising their teaching ministry as Catholic Bishops in a pluralistic democracy, seeking to contribute to the public debate, seeking to inform, seeking to raise the moral issue explicitly in the public debate. They do not claim that no one else has ever done this; they do not even claim that they know how to raise it in the best possible way. But I think they are very much taken with the responsibility to insure that the moral issues get raised as a major element in the public debate, along with political, strategic, and technical questions. As a teaching document, it reflects the moral pluralism I have outlined, and it also descends to specifics in the policy area. Perhaps the current draft doesn't make clear enough what was very clear to the drafting committee, that when you move from moral principles to specifying those principles in terms of policy, choices, and cases, increasing specificity yields decreasing certitude. And, in terms of traditional categories of Catholic moral theology, increasing specificity yields decreasing binding force on the consciences of the community of faith. That does not mean that it carries no force, or exerts no authority; it is simply a recognition that being more specific means being less certain and thus less authoritative. But they do descend to specifics in terms of the use of nuclear weapons (they give three cases), and also in terms of deciding about deterrence. Their judgment on deterrence is made principally in reference to the Pope's statement in June, while the debate that preceded that earlier statement is very much in evidence in the Bishops' document. They affirm the Pope's judgment about the moral acceptability of deterrence under limited conditions, but they lay great stress on the limits, which is not surprising, since many of them have grappled with this particular question for a long time. They are dubious about accepting the arguments for deterrence, but in the end they affirm the need for deterrence within strict limits, what one might call a marginal justification. They are aware that they have opened an argument rather than closed it. They know that this is a new stage to what was begun with *Gaudium et spes,* but they do want to come to judgment and not just ask questions.

Finally, there is the relationship of public policy and personal choice. There has been a great deal of concern about whether the Bishops are going to try to issue orders to people in this document. They have designed the last part of the Letter in the form of a series of statements to various people, principally to the American Catholic community precisely as the American Catholic community, arguing that the question of nuclear arms must be a significant moral and political question for every Catholic citizen, indeed for every citizen. There is no attempt to "target" people in specific vocations, if I may use a rather inept analogy at this point. They begin in this final section by speaking to the community of citizens. Within that community, there are clearly individuals whose professions, vocations, and responsibilities raise very specific questions in this area, and the Bishops try to address them. The style of address is to reaffirm principles binding on everyone, to highlight certain issues where these principles become particularly significant, and then to call people to form their consciences in a mature adult way, in freedom and with responsibility. In this they are following very closely the style of teaching initiated by the Second Vatican Council.

This is as far as they go in terms of specificity. Now there are statements in the document such as: "No Christian may rightly obey orders that include the direct killing of civilians." But this is hardly an invention of the American Bishops. It is as old as the tradition on noncombatant immunity, and if they reaffirm it, they have not invented it. Thus their style at this point seems to me clearly postconciliar, both in terms of the moral analysis of questions opened up by *Gaudium et spes,* but also in terms of their approach to the questions of personal choice, teaching authority, and professional and civic responsibility.

In conclusion, I think it is important to stress that this is the Bishops' Letter, but not yet the Church's letter. For the Bishops are only part of the Church. The debate that is going on already and will certainly continue when the letter is published will determine whether the Bishops' Letter becomes the Church's letter, and what impact that will have on our wider society. Some people have argued that the process is as important as the product. I am open to that interpretation just so long as it does not undercut the need for a product. But it is a peculiarly American Catholic debate, both in terms of the nature of the issue, the nuclear question, and in terms of the style in which it has been and could continue to be carried on: pluralistic but not antinomian, and democratic in the sense that it opens the debate for the whole Church. If we carry it out well, it will be a contribution not only to the community of faith but to the full community as well, and, one hopes, to the universal Church.

Discussion

Q: Does the Bishops' Letter address a "no first use" policy recommended by Bundy, McNamara, and Kennan, or does it go beyond it to what we might call a "no use" policy?

A: In the section on use, there are three cases that are distinguished. The first describes what might be called counterpopulation use, and the Bishops outlaw that on the basis of the argument that direct attacks on noncombatants constitute murder. The second case is what they call the "initiation of nuclear warfare." In the political debate, that is more properly known, I suppose, as the "no first use" argument, but they don't use that terminology. They do address the question, however, and argue against first use as crossing a nuclear barrier without sufficient political and moral justification. They distinguish a third case which they call limited nuclear exchange, which is meant not so much to get into the no-first-use debate, but the other debate, which has been going on since Henry Kissinger wrote about it in 1957, on the question of limited nuclear warfare in Europe. And, once again, the Bishops attempt to draw a line against use on the basis of a prudential calculus.

But if you ask me to use classical moral categories, if you ask me whether they say using a nuclear weapon is intrinsically evil, for example, the answer is that they don't use a statement like that. In fact, they don't cover every single case of use. There is indeed a deliberate ambiguity in the letter which reflects a deliberate ambiguity in all of the literature about deterrence. But as far as use goes, they argue against it in the three instances I have given. The thrust of the letter is to place in doubt the notion that nuclear weapons can be controlled, and this doubt is based on prudential considerations drawn from the social sciences and the scientific community, rather than from specifically ethical data. Still, one cannot find in the letter a single sentence that sums up an absolute moral position on the use of nuclear weapons, but the thrust of the whole letter is clearly against crossing the nuclear barrier.

Q: I'm interested in what you've said about the process being an American Catholic process, and the document an American Catholic document. From everything I've heard about the letter, I'd agree with that. My question is, did the Bishops intend it to be that way, and are they comfortable with it? Also, have they received any signals from the more universal Church of uneasiness with their positions?

A: A very good question. I think they are comfortable with the ideal, though they know they're dealing with an issue which is much larger than the American Catholic dialogue. Secondly, we have tried to solicit signals from the rest of the Church. The first draft of the document went out in June of 1982 to a number of episcopal conferences. We focused on Europe, but it was also sent to the Latin American Bishops' Conference; and, of course, it was sent to the Holy See for careful scrutiny. And I can tell you that it was given far more than a casual glance there! We have had responses from the European Bishops and from the Holy See. So far, the European Bishops have responded to the first draft, and we are waiting for responses to the second. They certainly have concerns, there's no question about that, and there is a meeting planned in Europe, probably in Rome, for early 1983 with members of some of the episcopal conferences. I see Fr. Frank Winters here; he has surveyed the European views on this question in the most recent issue of *Theological Studies* (September 1982) rather completely, reviewing certain of the differences. But the consultation will continue.

Q: This is more of a comment than a question. I really find it hard to understand the moral pluralism of the document as you describe it, while on other prolife issues, like abortion, there does not seem to be any pluralism; there is a clear categorical judgment about not taking life. Secondly, as I read the gospel and the Christian tradition, there is a clear nonviolent bias there, and Christians are called upon to overcome evil by doing good.

A: I tried to argue that there is indeed a relationship between the abortion issue and the war issue. But I think the relationship is that of analogy rather than identity. And since they're not identical issues, you don't want to get into a kind of lock-step approach, so that your answer to one is the same as the answer to the other. In moral matters, consistency yields analogous judgments among a variety of issues. You have the common themes of respecting human life, protecting innocent life, not directly attacking innocent life, and these run through the abortion issue and the war issue. But the total fabric of the moral issue in each case is not exactly the same. That doesn't mean that you might not come out with a "pacifist" view in both cases, but I don't think it is self-evident that you must.

Secondly, as you know, the tradition manifested clearly a

strong nonviolent character in the early Church, but the literature I've been able to pursue on that question indicates that we have more clarity on the fact that the majority of the Church was nonviolent than we have on the reasons why they were nonviolent. With Augustine, the argument underwent a shift, but it wasn't a shift from doing good to doing evil. Augustine and others argued that although it was tragic, it was still morally right to take life under certain circumstances. So, with that change in the tradition, one enters into an argument about how you do the good in situations that are conflicted. And that is where the moral pluralism comes from, it seems to me.

Q: I'd like to take a slightly different approach to this question. Assuming, as I think we should, that the Catholic Church does not have the same impact on public opinion in the Soviet Union as it does here, don't you think you're placing an unfair burden on the Reagan administration to reduce arms when, at the same time, the Soviet Union is not under the same pressure from public opinion? In the long run, might that imbalance have a destabilizing effect with the Soviet Union, requiring something approaching unilateral disarmament on our part, while the Soviet Union goes on without having to worry about similar demands?

A: First of all, the letter is not aimed primarily at the Reagan administration. I think to read it that way would be to take a mistaken view of the letter. The letter is rather addressed to American policy, and, to take one already noted example, the policy of no first use has been in place for 38 years and is thus not specifically related to the current administration. Do the Bishops hope to have an impact on the current administration? Clearly they do, and indeed the letter has been drafted with a view to the long term, so that it will have an impact on administrations to come as well.

Secondly, obviously there is not the same kind of impact on public opinion in the United States and in the Soviet Union. But I wouldn't say that there's no impact at all. Again, the Bishops think of themselves as working in conjunction with the Holy Father, and we should note that when he sent his delegation to President Reagan, he sent one to the Soviet leadership as well. Pope John Paul is not without impact in Eastern Europe, I am told, and so the Church's impact on this question is not as unilateral as it might seem.

Thirdly, the question of destabilization is one of those very tricky issues in the arms race today. What is stabilizing and destabilizing can be argued about for a long time. Is it stabilizing, for instance, not to cap the qualitative developments in the arms race? Was it in fact a stabilizing factor to proceed with MIRV in 1971 when we took the lead in that development and did not table a MIRV ban in the SALT I discussion for a number of reasons? Inevitably, the Soviets followed suit, and now we've got the "window of vulnerability" which is leading us to produce the MX. Is that kind of logic a stabilizing or destabilizing factor? Thus, it seems to me that the question about what constitutes stabilizing and destabilizing moves is very much open to discussion. The Bishops are clearly saying that they agree with you that the arms race is an interacting pattern. Who leads whom is always an open question, but there's clearly this pattern of interaction, and they would like to place some reasonable restraints and establish a clear direction for the arms race for at least one of the actors, precisely with the hope of influencing the whole process. Finally, they do not call for unilateral disarmament. They do call for what is described as independent initiatives which are then defined rather precisely: these are steps on which you could get an agreement, a consensus of experts that certain measures could be taken without serious detriment to our deterrent capability. Moreover, you take these steps for a defined period of time, and if there is no reciprocity, no response, you are no longer bound by those steps. That is not unilateralism in any significant sense; rather it is a calculated attempt to turn the dynamics of the arms race around.

Q: As far as the political import of the Bishops' statement goes, it seems that their statements on Central America, especially El Salvador, have not had as great an impact as this message on nuclear deterrence. How do you explain that, especially with regard to statements on domestic issues?

A: Let me try and give you my assessment of what impact the Bishops' statements on Central America have had. There is a distinction in strategic literature between deterrence and compellence, and I think the function of the Bishops' Central American statements has been the area of deterrence. What I mean is that they may have prevented some things from happening, questioned the logic of a certain kind of policy, raised and set limits for such a policy. We've had much less success in the area of compellence, that is, for changing the nature of the policy itself. There has been some impact there, but not nearly enough, I think.

    Secondly, I think there is a variety of reasons why statements on nuclear deterrence have had a much greater impact. One reason, I think, is that there is a much broader spectrum of the Bishops' Conference directly involved in this issue than in Central America. On Central America, most of the Bishops have been involved in support of the national Conference rather than individually, whereas, on the nuclear question, they are supporting a national position which they're trying to work out as a group, but many of them have also been involved very directly in a personal way. Moreover, the dynamics of the American political process on the arms question is rather different from the dynamics of the Central American question. I think it is fair to say that when the Bishops took their position on Central America in 1981, there weren't many other major institutions taking a similar position on the American political scene. Obviously, there's a whole series of major institutions and groups taking positions on the arms race, so that the Bishops are involved in a wider framework even though they are attempting to make their own specific contribution.

Q: I have a question on the timing of the document, because I think it is crucial to some of the criticism that we are hearing right now. The American nuclear arsenal was built up in the late 1960s and early 1970s. At that time the strategic doctrine was "counter-value," that is, mutually assured destruction; by the pastoral standards of the Bishops and in most peoples' view, that is a far more barbaric policy than what has evolved recently. Weren't the Bishops rather complacent about speaking out earlier? I realize there was not a grass-roots consensus, nor had the Holy See discussed the matter the way it has discussed it recently. Still, we've seen the nuclear problem evolve over two decades to where it is now, and weren't the Bishops under an obligation to speak up before this?

A: I think that your case could easily be made. In fact, I don't think you'd find many people who would dispute it. The fact is that the consensus was simply not there for such a document in an earlier time. Between a third and a half of the current bishops have been appointed within the last ten years, and so you are dealing with a very different group of people. Let me be very specific here. There is no Cardinal Spellman in this hierarchy; there was previously. That is simply a fact, not a detrimental statement about anyone, but a classification of position. At this time you do not have a man of his stature *and* of his position. The Bishops who represent his position do not have his stature; and the Bishops who do have his stature do not hold to the same position.

Secondly, you have now a clear sense of a collegial engagement of the Bishops in this issue. I have no doubt that the so-called "Pax Christi Bishops" have been one of the moving forces in creating this consensus. They haven't been the only force, and it's unlikely, I think, that the final version will come out exactly as they would have written it, but they have been a potent force. In an earlier time, in the late fifties and early sixties, the opportunity to create such a consensus was not present.

Thirdly, in the pre-Vatican II, preconciliar model of the Church, the notion that foreign policy was the business of the local hierarchies was not a strongly shared assumption. The U.S. Catholic Bishops' Conference has been involved in domestic questions since right after World War I, but the message from Rome was quite clear that foreign policy was well taken care of by the Holy See. So there was no strong sense that a local Church should deal with a foreign policy issue. All these factors contributed to a situation in which the Bishops were not deeply enough involved in the issue to be moved to address the question of nuclear arms.

Q: From everything I've read about the Bishops' Letter, I think it is a very important contribution, but there's one problem that hasn't been resolved, I feel. From what I've read, the document offers a justification for accumulating nuclear weapons on the ground of deterrence. And it is precisely on the basis of deterrence that continuation and accumulation of atomic weapons is being urged. Yet, deterrence itself represents a danger to peace in that the accumulation of nuclear weapons poses a threat for nations that do not accept our understanding of deterrence. Historically, too, we've threatened other nations that did not possess atomic weapons with the use of the same. I'm afraid that justification of deterrence takes away significantly from the affirmative impact of the Bishops' statement.

A: Pascal once said there are certain questions that take you by the throat, and you have just grabbed me by the throat. What I mean is that the deterrence question is by far the toughest issue in the document. Certain Bishops spoke to it this morning, and they didn't all take the same point of view by any means. One Bishop said he wanted more clarity in the matter, and, I confess, my instinctive comment under my breath was: Do you think there is any more clarity on the issue? I'm not sure how much clearer you can get on this question.

On the other hand, I don't think the logic of the document falls into the trap that you mention. I'm not saying that the Bishops have solved the question, but they do make a clear distinction between providing marginal justification for the concept of deterrence and legitimating everything that is proposed under the heading of deterrence. As I said, there is some division of opinion, but I think the most compelling reason for handling the deterrence question the way they do is that you can't simply ignore the notion that, to some degree, possession does prevent use. You might doubt it, but you can't simply disregard it. Thus, to dismiss the theory of deterrence on moral grounds involves a factual judgment about which there is legitimate dispute.

Still, even as they provide marginal justification for deterrence, they go on to articulate a series of principles or judgments for determining what elements should not be included in deterrence, and they ask what steps ought to be taken within the framework of deterrence to make it more secure, to reduce its size and scope, and to control its role in international politics. All of this, I think, is implicit in the document. The Bishops are not trying to provide legitimation for everything. For certain people, that is not enough; they feel that what is required is a clear condemnation of the very idea of deterrence. This is the hard case, this is where the debate will continue to be argued between these two points of view: that is, between the position that is in the document today, and the view that the Bishops ought to condemn deterrence straight out. That's where the argument remains for the future.

The Georgetown Leadership Seminar is a gathering of selected leaders from around the world. It was established in 1982 by senior academicians, government officials, and businessmen associated with Georgetown University to promote dialogue among individuals who will shape the future of their countries and the world. The Seminar is sponsored by the oldest and largest school of its type in the world as part of its commitment to intercultural education for foreign service in public and private sector interests. Launching of the Seminar was made possible by grants from Nissan Motor Corporation, Korf Industries, Inc., the German Marshall Fund, the United States Information Agency, and the Carl A. Weyerhauser Trust.

This publication is sponsored by the Seminar in the interest of promoting the widest possible exchange of views among young leaders about the future and the values and ethical perspectives which will help shape it.

Program Committee

Dr. Madeleine Albright
Donner Professor of International Studies
School of Foreign Service
Cathleen Black
Publisher, *New York Magazine*
The Honorable Zbigniew Brzezinski
Senior Advisor, Center for Strategic and International Studies
Dr. Bart Fisher, Esq.
Patton, Boggs, and Blow; Adjunct Professor of International Affairs, School of Foreign Service
Dr. Allan Goodman
Associate Dean, School of Foreign Service (co-director)
The Honorable Henry Kissinger
University Professor of Diplomacy, School of Foreign Service
Dr. Peter Krogh
Dean, School of Foreign Service (co-director)
Dr. R. Gerald Livingston
Research Professor, German Studies Program
School of Foreign Service
The Honorable Donald McHenry
University Research Professor, Georgetown University
Richard Millman, Esq.
Washington, DC
Dr. Theodore Moran
Director, Landegger Program in International Business Diplomacy, School of Foreign Service

The Honorable David Newsom
Associate Dean, School of Foreign Service and Director,
Institute for the Study of Diplomacy
Dr. Edward Sanders
Staff Director, Senate Foreign Relations Committee
Yasuhiko Suzuki
Vice President, External Relations
Nissan Motor Corporation
The Honorable Viron P. Vaky
Research Professor of Diplomacy
School of Foreign Service